ROMANO GUARDINI

MEDITATIONS BEFORE MASS

and

SACRED SIGNS

"I am thrilled to see these texts, modern classics by any standard, come back to life in this newly published format. Amidst past and present controversies about the Mass, these little works remind us that the best place to start if we want a more fulfilling experience of the liturgy is with ourselves, in acts of loving and disciplined attentiveness that can help the mystery of our redemption take deeper root in our hearts and so also in our lives. Highly recommended."

John C. Cavadini
Director of the McGrath Institute for Church Life
University of Notre Dame

"Romano Guardini's work, inspired by the Holy Spirit, deeply impacts how I think and communicate about the liturgy. His insights help me 'begin again' as I seek to pray the Mass with my whole being. I am confident they will do the same for you."

Sr. Alicia Torres, FE
National Eucharistic Revival Executive Team

"These two great works want you to encounter Jesus Christ in the materiality of the Church's worship and thereby learn a more responsible way of being human."

From the foreword by Timothy P. O'Malley
Director of Education, McGrath Institute for Church Life
University of Notre Dame

ROMANO GUARDINI'S

MEDITATIONS BEFORE MASS

and

SACRED SIGNS

Two Spiritual Classics

Foreword by Timothy P. O'Malley

Christian Classics ✠ Notre Dame, Indiana

Meditation before Mass first published in English in 1956 by Newman Press. Translated by Elinor Castendyk Briefs.

Sacred Signs first published in English in 1956 by Pio Decimo Press. Translated by Grace Branham.

Foreword © 2024 by Timothy P. O'Malley

Founded in 1865, Ave Maria Press is a ministry of the United States Province of Holy Cross.

www.avemariapress.com/christian-classics

Paperback: ISBN-13 978-0-87061-322-7

E-book: ISBN-13 978-0-87061-323-4

Cover images © e55evu / iStock / Getty Images Plus and sedmak / iStock / Getty Images Plus.

Cover design by Samantha Watson.

Text design by David Scholtes.

Printed and bound in the United States of America.

for

Lene and Hans Waltmann

CONTENTS

Foreword

by Timothy P. O'Malley

Few persons were more important to the renewal of Catholic intellectual and spiritual life in the twentieth century than Servant of God Fr. Romano Guardini (1885–1968). Guardini was a philosopher, a theologian, an interpreter of literature, an intellectual historian, a cultural critic, and a composer of spiritual classics. If you want to understand the return to the sources of scripture and tradition *(ressourcement)* undertaken at the Second Vatican Council, there is no better figure to read than Guardini—who taught and influenced many of the most important theological thinkers of the twentieth century.

Still, and perhaps because it's my own discipline, I have a particular affection for Guardini's liturgical works. In the early twentieth century, Guardini wrote several texts related to liturgical formation. In 1918 he composed *The Spirit of the Liturgy*, laying out the various theological and philosophical principles required for fruitful participation in the liturgy. In 1922 he wrote *Sacred Signs*—a spiritual meditation on the physical signs used in the Church's worship. In 1923 he released *Liturgical Formation*, in which he laid out a comprehensive program for the formation of human beings in the liturgical act. His *Meditations before Mass* (1939) applied his approach to liturgical contemplation to the various actions and prayers of the Eucharistic liturgy.

An astute reader will notice that each of these works were written well before the liturgical reforms of the Second Vatican Council (1963–1968). Guardini did not live to see the reformed Eucharistic rites of the Church, which were promulgated two years after his death. Guardini was not against these reforms, but he properly understood that such liturgical reform would have little impact if one ignored the deeper malaise around the liturgy precipitated by modernity. As he wrote in a letter to the German bishops during the Second Vatican Council:

> What is being discussed is thus the question of whether this marvelously opened liturgical possibility can be realized to the full extent. Maybe it will be exhausted by removing aberrations or will be satisfied by creating something new, by giving better instructions about what acts and things mean, or by the renewed opportunity to learn a forgotten act and retain long forgotten attitudes. (Romano Guardini, "The Cultic Act and the Contemporary Act of Liturigcal Formation," in Liturgy and Liturgical Formation, trans. Jan Bentz [Chicago: Liturgy Training Publications, 2022], 3.)

The liturgical crisis, for Guardini, was not caused by the rites of the Church (either pre- or post-conciliar). Instead, it was a forgetfulness within the Church about how to engage in the liturgical act. A sacramental amnesia, you could call it. No one understands how to walk in a procession. We can't meditate upon a candle because we have grown used to electric light. The marvelous dimensions of bread and wine, as Eucharistic elements, have been forgotten.

Guardini's liturgical classics are, therefore, closely linked to his critique of modernity. Guardini is no traditionalist. But he does recognize that the technological innovations of the modern age have changed what it means to be human. His mid-1920s *Letters from Lake Como* describe these changes. Once upon a time, we humans were close to the natural order. Yes, we harnessed the power of wind to move sails. But the scale of those ships was humane. It required a human body to move the mast, to catch the wind in the right way to move forward. With the steam engine, we no longer need the wind, and our ships have become almost like monsters moving across the waters. With electric light, we no longer need the candle. How can we appreciate the quality of natural light that illuminates a room in an age where a mere flip of the switch does the same?

Guardini is not a Romantic. He recognizes that there is no going back, the creation of a utopian community where we traverse the sea only by sail or illuminate our homes exclusively through natural light is not in the offing. But he does recognize that to rightly engage the liturgical act, we must know how to be creatures. For that we need liturgical formation or education. Guradini used the German word *bildung*, which encompasses both of these things.

Knowing how to be creatures means that we must remember what it means to be human. What it means to employ our bodies in the act of worship and how to relate to matter as the deepest expression of our hopes and dreams. Guardini's writings constantly invite us to pay attention. His *Liturgical Formation* begs us to get into the natural world, to go hiking again, and to recognize what it means to move our bodies in the context of a world infused with the glory of God.

In none of this does Guardini embrace a pantheism where God is present in the created order as another object. His focus, even in *Sacred Signs*, is never on the world alone. Rather, in his thought, he always interrupts with the revelation of the Word made flesh, Jesus Christ, who transformed what it means to be creatures. A candle is never a candle alone. It is a living sign of Jesus Christ. An altar is no mere table. Here is the sacrificial presence of the crucified and risen God-man. All things have been restored in Christ.

Guardini's approach to liturgical formation is desperately needed in our own day where our amnesia has only become more acute. It is why Pope Francis regularly invokes Guardini in his writings on sacraments, ecology, and liturgical celebration. You want to make an impact on climate change, Pope Francis wonders. Yes, you could probably institute some policies that would help with this. But you also need to relate to time and space in a more humane way, to learn that the human person is not made for production. The Sabbath rest of Sunday intervenes—spend time beholding rather than producing. Learn from Guardini, Pope Francis invites us in *Laudato Si'*.

That is, discover anew that liturgical formation wasn't about changing the rites around, which seemed to be the sometimes-almost-exclusive fascination of liturgists in the twentieth century. In the end, Vatican II wasn't about whether the priest faces the people or not. It wasn't about the use of the vernacular or not. It was about a new way of being human that took very seriously wisdom drawn from the liturgical and sacramental rites of the Church.

Guardini, of course, couldn't have imagined our own age where we seem even more removed from a humane way of living. The progress of industry has been replaced by constant technological innovation. Digital devices that promise salvation. An addiction to speed where every one of our phones is obsolete within days of being purchased, and that same speed can easily lead to the elimination of the dignity of work as each of us are replaced with robots and artificial intelligence that can perhaps better and more efficiently accomplish our jobs. Men and women have forgotten how to be, to gaze upon the created order instead of mediating all experience through cell phones. We use this power to harm creation and to get rid of or isolate human beings who get in the way of so-called progress and productivity such as the unborn, the seriously ill, the criminals, the addicts, and the elderly. After all, it's every man and woman for themselves—do we really need community?

What are we to do? Yes, there's a role for politics and advocacy in all of this. But as Pope Francis himself notes in *Laudato Si'*, retrieving Guardini, the liturgical-sacramental life of the Church still has something to offer. Learn to listen to a bell again and to remember your embodiment as you hold your hands aright in prayer. Come to terms with the intimacy that God desires with your flesh and blood self, willing to feed you with himself under the signs of bread and wine.

Guardini, in the two works of this book, is inviting each of us to take responsibility for a liturgical education that has the potentiality of renewing the cosmos and our personal histories alike. *Meditations before Mass* and *Sacred Signs* are not only about preparing you to understand better what happens at Mass. These two great works want you to encounter Jesus Christ in the materiality of the Church's worship and thereby learn a more responsible way of being human—a liturgical way of being a man or a woman, a creature made for worshipful wisdom.

The educational approach of both these works requires slow, repetitive reading. Don't think that by reading these works once, even twice, that you can implement a program in your parish that will change everything. Such an assumption falls prey to the very technocratic culture (one that I fear the US Church is intoxicated by, based on our addiction to strategic planning and activity) that Guardini seeks to deconstruct. The task of living a worshipful life is a lifelong project.

So, think about reading these two works (often and slowly) as prophetic assaults against an anti-contemplative, anti-sacramental, and anti-liturgical culture. Waste time reading these before Mass. After Mass. In between Masses. Learn from Guardini to be present to the God who comes to us through sacred signs. Through Guardini's contemplation, think about a different way of living, one grounded in the Church's liturgy.

And who knows? Maybe in fifteen years, we'll have *finally* stopped fighting about the liturgy in the United States (we can hope, right?). Instead, we'll have learned to live a liturgical life, one that makes the world more sacred. More humane.

A liturgical world. The one that God created in the first place.

Timothy P. O'Malley, PhD

Director of Education, McGrath Institute for Church Life

University of Notre Dame

Meditations
before
Mass

INTRODUCTION

The chapters of this book originated as discourses held before Holy Mass in order to prepare for its celebration. They made no attempt to interpret the essence of the Lord's memorial or to narrate his life; their purpose was simply to reveal what the Mass demands of us and how those demands may be properly met.

For many a believer the Mass has assumed the character of a sacred spectacle or of some mysterious proceeding before which he says his prayers. Its reality consequently is buried, and something irreplaceable is lost. The reasons for this are many and go so far back that criticism is pointless. But it is time that the Mass become again for the faithful what it is and was instituted to be: the sacred action of Christ's community, which, though under the care of the priestly office, is meant to live and act as a true community, as the Acts of the Apostles (2:46) and the first Epistle to the Corinthians (11:17–34) point out. That is where this book is meant to help. It does not try to show how the Mass should be celebrated or how, within the prescribed limits of ecclesiastical law (or perhaps through a more perfect fulfillment of the *lex orandi*), the organic structure of the sacred ceremony could be brought out more clearly, or even how closer participation of the faithful is to be achieved. That is the task of a religious manual. What is needed here is personal preparation for Holy Mass. This requires not only "Mass preparation" in the usual sense of the individual believer strengthening his faith, purifying his heart, arranging and direct-ing his intentions, but also that fundamental, vital attitude absolutely necessary to transform a collection of individuals into a congregation, and a restless crowd into a "holy people" in the sight of God. Only from such central preparedness can the gaze lifted to the altar grow inwardly quiet and receptive to holiness; only then can hearing and speaking in church differ from the give and take of words in the street, the home, or the office.

Part One of our study will be concerned exclusively with these basic aspects. Its task is important as it is modest. Until it has been accomplished, all discussion of the liturgy remains on the level of intellectual exercise or aesthetic sensation, and use of the missal will help as little as establishment of the Dialogue Mass. If the liturgical act is to be taken seriously, we must prepare for it beforehand with the total concentration of mind and heart.

Part Two will discuss the Mass itself, inquiring into its essence and what it means to us—but always keeping in mind what it demands of us. We refer not only to the usual interpretation of those demands: that we participate eagerly in the sacred ceremony, that we make a real effort to conform our attitude to that which sustains the Eucharist, thus practicing self-restraint and sacrifice. All this is very important, but our problem here is quite different; how must we cooperate in the celebration of the Mass so that it really becomes what it is essentially: a holy, liturgical act? Faith, love, and readiness for sacrifice are the greatest ideals that exist and a completely unliturgical "Mass devotion" can doubtless effect true Christian service before God. But what we are aiming at is also important and deserves the utmost attention.

We remarked previously that we were concerned here not with knowing but with doing. This is not entirely true. There are different roads to knowledge, and one that usually suggests itself first is the road of contemplation, penetration, comparison, and conclusion. Much can be grasped by these means, but not everything. I can, for example, perceive things which exist in themselves but not those intangibles which first come into being through doing. To achieve knowledge of the latter I must do them. Through study I can learn the kinds of trees or ascertain the pattern of community life around me, but study cannot teach me what fidelity or love mean, at least not their ultimate senses—what they mean for me.

Mere observation and consideration can prepare me to discuss trees or the phenomena of society with a certain competence; but my words grow thin and empty the moment I attempt similar "observations" on matters of the heart. If I really want to know what fidelity is, I must practice it. I can speak with authority about love only if in some form or other I have accepted its challenge. And it is the same here. Up to a certain point I can understand the nature of Holy Mass by studying the Bible and missal or by reading books on the history of the liturgy. But its essence, the act in all the earnestness of salvation, the *doing* in his memory, is mine only when I also "do." Possibly the true nature of the Mass is so feebly established in the Christian consciousness in spite of catechism, sermon, and much pious literature, because the believers rarely "do" it properly. If this book helps toward better doing, deeper understanding will follow.

Romano Guardini

Part One

Sacred Bearing

1. STILLNESS

When Holy Mass is properly celebrated there are moments in which the voices of both priest and faithful become silent. The priest continues to officiate as the rubrics indicate, speaking very softly or refraining from vocal prayer; the congregation follows in watchful, prayerful participation.[1] What do these intervals of quiet signify? What must we do with them? What does *stillness* really imply?

It implies above all that speech ends and silence prevail, that no other sounds—of movements, of turning pages, of coughing and throat-clearing—be audible. There is no need to exaggerate. Men live, and living things move; a forced outward conformity is no better than restlessness. Nevertheless, stillness is still, and it comes only if seriously desired. If we value it, it brings us joy—if not, discomfort. People are often heard to say: "But I can't help coughing" or "I can't kneel quietly"; yet once stirred by a concert or lecture they forget all about coughing and fidgeting. That stillness proper to the most beautiful things in existence dominates, a quiet area of attentiveness in which the beautiful and truly important reign. We must earnestly desire stillness and be willing to give something for it; then it will be ours. Once we have experienced it, we will be astounded that we were able to live without it.

Moreover, stillness must not be superficial, as it is when there is neither speaking nor squirming; our thoughts, our feelings, our hearts must also find repose. Then genuine stillness permeates us, spreading ever deeper through the seemingly plumbless world within.

Once we try to achieve such profound stillness, we realize that it cannot be accomplished all at once. The mere desire for it is not enough; we must practice it. The minutes before Holy Mass are best; but in order to have them for genuine preparation we must arrive early. These are not times for gazing or daydreaming or for unnecessary thumbing of pages, but for inwardly collecting and calming ourselves.[2] It would be better still to begin on our way to church. After all, we are going to a sacred celebration. Why not let the commute there be an exercise in composure, a kind of overture to what is to come? I would even suggest that preparation for holy stillness really begins the day before. Liturgically, Saturday evening already belongs to the Sunday. If for instance, after suitable reading we were to collect ourselves for a brief period of composure, its effects the next day would be evident.

Thus far we have discussed stillness negatively: no speech and no sound. But it is much more than the absence of these, a mere gap, as it were, between words and sounds—stillness itself is something positive. Of course we must be able to appreciate it as such. There is sometimes a pause in the midst of a lecture or a service or some public function. Almost invariably someone promptly coughs or clears his throat. He is experiencing stillness as a breach in the unwinding road of speech and sound, which he attempts to fill with something, anything. For him the stillness was only a lacuna, a void which gave him a sense of disorder and discomfort. Actually, it is something rich and brimming.

Stillness is the tranquility of the inner life—the quiet at the depths of its hidden stream. It is a collected, total presence, a being "all there," receptive, alert, ready. There is nothing inert or oppressive about it.

Attentiveness is the clue to the stillness in question, the stillness before God.

What then is a *church*? It is, to be sure, a building having walls, pillars, space. But these express only part of the word *church*, its shell. When we say that Holy Mass is celebrated "in church," we are including something more: the *congregation*. A congregation is not merely people. Churchgoers arriving, sitting, or kneeling in pews are not necessarily a congregation; they can be simply a roomful of more or less pious individuals. Congregation is formed only when those individuals are present not only corporally but also spiritually, when they have contacted one another in prayer and stepped together into the spiritual "space" around them, and strictly speaking, when they have first widened and heightened that space by prayer. Then true congregation comes into being, which, along with the building that is its architectural expression, forms the vital church in which the sacred act is accomplished. All this takes place only in stillness; out of stillness grows the real sanctuary. It is important to understand this. Church buildings may be lost or destroyed; then everything depends on whether or not the faithful are capable of forming congregations that erect indestructible "churches" wherever they happen to find themselves, no matter how poor or dreary their quarters. We must learn and practice the art of constructing spiritual cathedrals.

We cannot take stillness too seriously. Not for nothing do these reflections on the liturgy open with it. If someone were to ask me what the liturgical life begins with, I should answer: with learning stillness. Without it, everything remains superficial, vain. Our understanding of stillness is nothing strange or aesthetic. Were we to approach stillness on the level of aesthetics of mere withdrawal into the ego, we should spoil everything. What we are striving for is something very grave, very important, and unfortunately sorely neglected; the prerequisite of the liturgical holy act.

2. Silence and the Word

In the preceding chapter we discussed stillness in the presence of God. Only in such stillness, can the congregation fundamental to the sacred ritual come into being. Only in stillness can the room in which Holy Mass is celebrated be exalted into a church. Hence the beginning of divine service is the creation of stillness. Stillness is intimately related to speech and the word.

The word is a thing of mystery, so volatile that it vanishes almost on the lip, yet so powerful that it decides fates and determines the meaning of existence. A frail structure shaped by fleeting sound, yet it contains the eternal: truth. Words come from within, rising as sounds fashioned by the organs of a man's body, as expressions of his heart and spirit. He utters them, yet he does not create them, for they already existed independently of him. One word is related to another; together they form the great unity of language, that empire of truth-forms in which a man lives.

The living word arranges itself in various onion-like layers. The outermost is that of simple communication: news or a command. These can be conveyed artificially, as they often are, by the printed word or some sound-apparatus that reproduces human speech. The syllables thus produced draw their significance from genuine language, and they answer specific needs well enough. But this superficial, often mechanical, level of words is not yet true speech, which exists only in proportion to the amount of inner conviction carried over from the speaker to that which is spoken. The more clearly his meaning is embodied in intelligible sounds, and the more fully his heart is able to express itself, the more truly does his speech become living word.

The inmost spirit lives by truth, by its recognition of what is and what has value. Man expresses this truth in words. The more fully he recognizes it, the better his speech and the richer his words. But truth can be recognized only from silence. The constant talker will never, or at least rarely, grasp truth. Of course even he must experience some truths, otherwise he could not exist. He does notice certain facts, observe certain relations, draw conclusions, and make plans. But he does not yet possess genuine truth, which comes into being only when the essence of an object, the significance of a relation, and what is valid and eternal in this world reveal themselves. This requires the spaciousness, freedom, and pure receptiveness of that inner "clean-swept room" silence alone can create. The constant talker knows no such room within himself; hence he cannot know truth. Truth, and consequently the reality of speech, depends upon the speaker's ability to speak and to be silent in turn.

But what of fervor, which lives on emotion and emotion's evaluation of the costliness and significance of things? Doesn't fervor pour the more abundantly into speech the more immediate the experience behind it? And doesn't that immediacy remain greatest the less one stops to think? That is true, at least for the moment. But it is also true that the person who talks constantly grows empty, and his emptiness is not only momentary. Feelings that are always promptly poured out in words are soon exhausted. The heart incapable of storing anything, of withdrawing into itself, cannot thrive. Like a field that must constantly produce, it is soon impoverished.

Only the word that emerges from silence is substantial and powerful. To be effective it must first find its way into open speech, though for some truths this is not necessary: those inexpressible depths of comprehension of one's self, of others, and of God. For these the experienced but unspoken suffices. For all others, however, the interior word must become exterior. Just as there exists a perverted variety of speech, "talk," there also exists a perverted silence, dumbness. Dumbness is just as bad as garrulity. It occurs when silence, sealed in the dungeon of a heart that has no outlet, becomes cramped and oppressive. The word breaks open the stronghold. It carries light into the darkness and frees what has been held captive. Speech enables a man to account for himself and the world and to overcome both. It indicates his place among others and in history. It liberates. Silence and speech belong together. The one presupposes the other. Together they form a unit in which the vital man exists, and the discovery of that unit's namelessness is strangely beautiful. We do know this: man's essence is enclosed in the sphere of silence/speech just as the whole earthly life is enclosed in that of light/darkness, day/night.

Consequently, even for the sake of speech we must practice silence. To a large extent the Liturgy consists of words which we address to and receive from God. They must not degenerate into mere talk, which is the fate of all words, even the profoundest and holiest, when they are spoken improperly. In the words of the liturgy, the truth of God and of redeemed man is meant to blaze. In them the heart of Christ, in whom the Father's love lives, and the hearts of his followers must find their full expression. Through the liturgical word our inwardness passes over into the realm of sacred openness, which the congregation and its mystery create before God. Even God's holy mystery, entrusted by Christ to his followers when he said, "As often as you shall do these things, in memory of me shall you do them," is renewed through the medium of human words. All this, then, must find room in the words of the Liturgy. They must be broad and calm and full of inner knowledge, which they are only when they spring from silence.

The importance of silence for the sacred celebration cannot be over-stressed—silence which prepares for it as well as that silence which establishes itself again and again during the ceremony. Silence opens the inner fount from which the word rises.

3. Silence and Hearing

Silence and speech are interdependent and together form the nameless unit that supports our spiritual life. But there is another element essential here: hearing.

Let us imagine for a moment a Dialogue Mass; Epistle and Gospel, indeed, a substantial part of the Mass is read aloud in English. What do those believers who love the liturgy and wish to participate in it as fully as possible do? They take their missals in hand and read along with the reader. They mean well, they are eager not to miss a word; yet how odd the whole situation is! There stands the reader, continuing the service that the deacon once performed. Solemnly he reads the sacred words, and the believers he is addressing read with him! Can this be a genuine form of the spiritual act? Obviously not. Something has been destroyed. Solemn reading requires listening, not simultaneous reading. Otherwise why read aloud at all? Our bookish upbringing is to blame for this unnaturalness. Most deplorably, it encourages people to read when they should listen. As a result, the fairytale has died and poetry has lost its power; for its resonant, wise, fervent, and festive language is meant to be heard, not read. In Holy Mass, moreover, it is a question not only of beautiful and solemn words, but of the divine word.

Perhaps at this point someone may protest: "But these are mere aesthetic details which matter very little. The main thing is that the believers receive and understand the word of God—whether by reading or hearing is of no import." As a matter of fact, this question is vital. In silent reading that frail and powerful reality called "word" is incomplete.

It remains unfinished, entangled in print, corporal; vital parts are still lacking. The hurrying eye brings fleeting images to the imagination; the intelligence gains but a hazy "comprehension," and the result is of small worth. What has been lost belongs to the essence of the liturgical event. No longer does the sacred word unfold in its full spiritual-corporal reality and soar through space to the listener, to be heard and received into his life. Would it be a loss if men ceased to convey their most fervent thoughts in living speech, and instead communicated with each other only in writing? Definitely. All the bodily vitality of the ringing word would vanish. In the realm of faith also the loss would be shattering. After all, Christ himself spoke of hearing. He never said: "He who has eyes to read, read!" This is no attempt to devaluate the written word, which in its place is good and necessary. However, it must not crowd out what is better, more necessary and beautiful: hearing, from which, as St. Paul tells us, springs faith (Rom 10:14).

Faith can, of course, be kindled from the written text, but the Gospel, the "glad tidings," gains its full power only when it is heard. Members of a reading age, we have forgotten this, and so thoroughly that it is now difficult for us to realize what we have lost. The whole word is not the printed, but the spoken, in which alone truth stands free. Only words formed by the human voice have the delicacy and power necessary to stir the depths of emotion, the seat of the spirit, the full sensitiveness of the conscience. Like the sacraments God's word is spiritual-corporal; like them it is meant to nourish the spirit in flesh-and-blood man, to work in him as power. To do this it must be whole. This consideration takes us still deeper. The saving God who came to us was the eternal Word. But that Word did not come in a blaze of spiritual illumination or as something suddenly appearing in a book. He "was made flesh," flesh that could be seen, heard, grasped with hands, as St. John so graphically insists in the opening lines of his first epistle. The same mystery continues in the living word of liturgical proclamation, and it is all-important that the connection remains vital.

The Word of God is meant to be heard, and hearing requires silence.

To be sure that the point is clear, let us put it this way: how may proper hearing be prevented? I could say something to a man sitting out of earshot, for example. Then I should have to speak louder in order to establish the physical connection. Or I could speak loudly enough, but if his attention is elsewhere, my remarks will go unheeded. Then I must appeal to him to listen. Perhaps he does listen, notes what I say, follows the line of thought, tries his best, and yet fails to understand. Something in him remains closed. He hears my reasons, follows them intellectually and psychologically; he would understand at once if they applied to someone else. In regard to himself, he fails to see the connection because his pride will not admit the truth; perhaps a secret voice warns him that, were he to admit it, he would have to change things in his life that he is unwilling to change. The more examples we consider, the more clearly we realize that hearing too exists on many levels, and we begin to suspect its importance when the Speaker is God. Not for nothing did our Lord say: "He who has ears to hear, let him hear" (Mt 11:15).

To have ears to hear requires grace, for God's word can be heard only by him whose ears God has opened. He does this when he pleases, and the prayer for truth is directed at that divine pleasure. But it also requires something that we ourselves desire and are capable of: being inwardly "present" by listening from the vital core of our being and unfolding ourselves to that which comes from beyond, to the sacred word. All this is possible only when we are inwardly still. In stillness alone can we really hear. When we come in from the outside our ears are filled with the racket of the city, the words of those who have accompanied us, the laboring and quarrelling of our own thoughts, the disquiet of our hearts' wishes and worries, hurts and joys. How are we possibly to hear what God is saying? That we listen at all is something—not everyone does! It is even better when we pay attention and make a real effort to understand what is being said. But all this is not yet that attentive stillness in which God's word can take root. This must be established before the service begins, if possible in the silence on the way to church, still better in a brief period of composure the evening before.

4. Composure

In the religious life silence is seldom discussed alone. Sooner or later its companion, composure, demands our attention. Silence overcomes noise and talk; composure is the victory over distractions and unrest. Silence is the quiet of a person who could be talking; composure is the vital, dynamic unity of an individual who could be divided by his surroundings, tossed to and fro by the myriad happenings of every day.

What then do we mean by composure? As a rule, a man's attention is broken into a thousand fragments by the variety of things and persons about him. His mind is restless; his feelings seek objects that are constantly changing; his desires reach out for one thing after another; his will is captured by a thousand intentions, often conflicting. He is harried, torn, and self-contradictory. Composure works in the opposite direction, rescuing man's attention from the sundry objects holding it captive and restoring unity to his spirit. It frees his mind from its many tempting claims and focuses it on one, the all-important. It calls the soul that is dispersed over myriad thoughts and desires, plans and intentions back to itself, re-establishing its depth.

All things seem to disquiet man. The phenomena of nature intrigue him; they attract and bind. But because they are natural, they have a calming, collecting influence as well. It is much the same with those realities that make up human existence: encounter and destiny, work and pleasure, sickness and accident, life and death. All make their demands on man, crowding him in and overwhelming him; but they also give him earnestness and weight. What is genuinely disastrous is the disorder and artificiality of present-day existence. We are constantly stormed by violent and chaotic impressions. At once powerful and superficial, they are soon exhausted, only to be replaced by others. They are immoderate and disconnected, the one contradicting, disturbing, and obstructing the other. At every step we find ourselves in the claws of purposes and cross-purposes that inveigle and trick us. Everywhere we are confronted by advertising that attempts to force things upon us we neither want nor really need. We are constantly lured from the important and profound to the distracting, interesting, piquant. This state of affairs exists not only around but within us. To a large extent man lives without depth, without a center, in superficiality and chance. No longer finding the essential within himself, he grabs at all sorts of stimulants and sensations; he enjoys them briefly, tires of them, recalls his own emptiness, and demands new distractions. He touches everything brought within easy reach of his mind by the constantly increasing means of transportation, information, education, and amusement, but he doesn't really absorb anything. He contents himself with having "heard about it"; he labels it with some current catchword and shoves it aside for the next. He is a hollow man and tries to fill his emptiness with constant, restless activity. He is happiest when in the thick of things, in the rush, noise, and stimulus of quick results and successes. The moment quiet surrounds him, he is lost.

This state makes itself felt generally, in the religious life, in church services, and in Holy Mass. Constant unrest is one of its earmarks. Then there is much gazing about, uncalled for kneeling down and standing up, reaching for this and that, fingering of apparel, coughing, and throat-clearing. Even when behavior remains outwardly controlled, an inner restlessness is clearly evident in the way people sing, listen, and respond—in their whole bearing. They are not really present; they do not vitally fill the room and hour. They are not composed.

Composure is more than freedom from scattered impressions and occupations. It is something positive; it is life in its full depth and power. Left to itself, life will always turn outward toward the multiplicity of things and events, and this natural inclination must be counter-balanced. Consider for a moment the nature of respiration. It has two directions: outward and inward. Both are vital; each is part of this elementary function of life and neither is all of it. The living organism that only exhaled, or inhaled, would soon suffocate. Composure is the spiritual man's "inhalation," by which, from deep within, he collects his scattered self and returns to his center.

Only the composed person is really someone. Only he can be seriously addressed as one capable of replying. Only he is genuinely affected by what life brings him, for he alone is awake, aware. And not only is he wide awake in the superficial sense of being quick to see and grab his advantage—this is a watchfulness shared also by birds and ants. What we mean is true awareness: that inner knowledge of the essential; that ability to make responsible decisions—sensitivity, readiness, and *joie de vivre*.

Once composure has been established, the liturgy is possible. Not before. It is not much use to discuss Holy Scripture, the deep significance of symbols, and the vitality of the liturgical renewal if the prerequisite of earnestness is lacking. Without it, even the liturgy deteriorates to something "interesting," a passing vogue. To participate in the liturgy seriously we must be mentally composed. But, like silence, composure does not create itself; it must be willed and practiced.[3]

Above all, we must get to church early in order to "tidy up" inwardly. We must have no illusions about our condition when we enter the church; we must frankly face our restlessness, confusion, and disorder. To be exact, we do not yet really exist as persons—at least not as persons God can address, expecting a fitting response. We are bundles of feelings, fancies, thoughts, and plans all at cross-purposes with each other. The first thing to do, is to quiet and collect ourselves. We must be able to say honestly: "Now I am here. I have only one thing to do: participate with my whole being in the only thing that counts—the sacred celebration. I am entirely ready."

Once we attempt this, we realize how terribly distraught we are. Our thoughts drag us in all directions: to the people we deal with (family, friends, adversaries), to our work, to our worries, to public events, and to private engagements. We must pull our thoughts back again and again and again, repeatedly calling ourselves to order. And when we see how difficult it is, we must not give up, but realize only the more clearly that it is high time we returned to ourselves.

But is it possible at all? Isn't man hopelessly given over to outward impressions, to the press of his desires, and to his own unrest? The question brushes the ultimate: the difference between man and animal. An animal is really bound by these things, unfree—though, we must hasten to add, protected by the orderly disposition of its instincts. An animal is never truly distracted. In the exact sense we were using, it can be neither distracted nor composed; it has not yet been confronted with this either/or. Its own nature determines its existence and requires it to be in order. Only man can be distracted, because something in his spirit reaches beyond mere nature. The spirit can turn to the things of the world and lose itself there; the same spirit can also overcome distraction and fight its way through to composure. There is something mysterious about the spirit, something relevant to eternity. Absolute rest and composure *is* eternity. Time is unrest and dispersion; eternity is rest and unity, not inactivity or boredom—only fools connect these with it. Eternity is the brimming fullness of life in the form of repose. Something of eternity is deep within us. Let's call it by the beautiful names the spiritual masters use: the "ground of the soul" or the "peak of the spirit." In the first it appears as the repose of the intrinsic, of depth; in the second as the tranquility of remoteness and the heights. This seed of eternity is within me, and I can count on its support. With its aid I can step out of the endless chase; I can dismiss everything that does not belong here in God's house; I can grow still and whole so that I can honestly reply to his summons: "Here I am, Lord."

5. Composure and Action

Just as proper speech and hearing emerge from silence, proper bearing and good action emerge only from composure.

Action too is more than mere external happening. It has innumerable levels, as many as life itself. There are purely external functions, such as turning on a light; if the switch clicks properly, the light burns without further ado. But if I am performing some real task, particularly something important, I must concentrate on it or there will be mistakes. In the various relations between people—service, friendship, love—in everything that belongs to the sphere of man and his work, work is genuine only in the degree that the doer inwardly participates in it. Colloquial speech has several telling expressions for this: he is "completely absorbed" in his work, or "His heart isn't in it." For I can do a thing, alone and unaided and still put very little of myself into it. My body goes through motions and some mental activity is exerted; but on the whole my mind is elsewhere and the work proceeds accordingly. The nobler and the more difficult or important the task to be accomplished, the more completely I must give it my attention, earnestness, eagerness, and love, participating in it from the heart and with all the creative élan of the mind. That is composure: heart and mind concentrated on the here and now, not off on daydreams; it is being "all here."

This is true of all action, but particularly true of that which concerns us here—the service performed before God. The liturgy is based on the fact of God's presence in the church, and begins with man's response to that presence. This is how it differs from private prayer, which can take place anywhere, at home or in a street or field. Primarily—and this is decisive—liturgy means service in the holy place. It is a great mystery, God's presence in a place, and demands as a response that we appear before that presence. There is a beautiful expression for this in Italian: "*faro atto di presenza*," to perform the act of *being present*. It is the beginning of everything. But one must be really present with body and mind and soul, with attention, reverence, and love. That is composure. Only he who is composed can have God's presence within him and appear before him to respond to his outpouring grace with adoration and love.

Composure also makes possible the proper outward bearing. People's behavior in church is often so lax that even at the risk of sounding exaggerated, or worse, of being misunderstood and evoking unnatural deportment, I must call attention to it. Many churchgoers simply don't seem to know where they are or what it is all about. A man's presence in church does not mean merely that his body is there rather than elsewhere. His "body" is the equivalent of himself, and being present is a vital act. There are people who can walk into a room, sit down, and little more seems to have happened than a chair has been occupied. Someone else can come in, and though he neither says nor does anything further, his presence is like a power. There are works of art in which this quiet power of presence is very strong; we have only to think of those medieval paintings which portray numbers of saints seated next to each other. They do nothing; hardly a gesture or word is exchanged, yet everything is vitally alive with their presence. To be present is more than to sit or kneel in place. It is an act of the spirit and expresses itself in one's whole bearing.

Much the same is true of our various movements and gestures. Is there anything more embarrassing than the manner in which some people, upon entering a church, after an anemic genuflection immediately flop into their seats? Isn't this precisely how they take their places on a park bench or at the movies? Apparently they have no idea where they are; for were they to call on someone important after church, they would behave quite differently. As for sitting itself, in church it signifies more than mere comfort; it is the position of attentive listening. Similarly, kneeling here is quite different from the position a hunter might assume while taking aim; it is the offering of our erect position to God. And again, standing in church is a more profound act than that of a mere halt while walking, or the attitude of expectant waiting: it is the bearing of reverence before the heavenly Lord. We can do these things convincingly only when we are fully conscious of what is taking place around us, and that awareness is ours only when we are self-collected and composed.

Equally elementary and self-understood, yet equally in need of vigilance, are our acts of looking and seeing. Later we shall discuss in more detail the importance of the visual act in the divine service. It means more than the bird's discovery of a kernel or the deer's cautious survey of a landscape. It is the act by which a man grasps the essence of an object that he sees before him. To see something is the first step toward sharing in it. Sometimes in the theater we come upon a face intent on the performance. The sight of another completely disarmed and self-forgotten can be so strong as to embarrass, and quickly we turn away. A man's eyes contain the whole man. To gaze full of faith at the altar means a great deal more than merely to look up in order to see how far the sacred ceremony has progressed. Once in the cathedral of Monreale in Sicily, I had the wonderful experience of watching the believers participate in the blessing of the fire and of the Paschal Candle on Easter Saturday. The ceremonies lasted over five hours and were not yet finished when I had to leave. The people had no books and they did not recite the rosary; they only gazed—but with all their souls. So much of this visual power has been lost. There are many reasons for this: the vast amount of reading we do and the countless impressions of city life, news services, and movies. Ultimately, they are largely to blame for the widespread loss of that composure which the simple man brought up and the Christian tradition still possesses. The gaze directed to the altar is exactly as profound as the composure from which it comes.

Or suppose we consider the gestures of the liturgy; for instance, the simplest and holiest of all: the sign of the cross. Isn't the way it is often made an out-and-out scandal? The careless, crippled greeting a man makes *en passant* to someone of indifferent interest? Certainly it is not the gesture with which we sign our bodies with the symbol of Christ's death and flood our souls with the vision of salvation, with which we acknowledge ourselves his and place ourselves under his power![4] Or consider the way people sometimes go up to receive Holy Communion. What an impression a non-believer who happens to be present (see 1 Cor 14:24) must receive at sight of certain believers on their way to the Lord's table—an impression either of a forced unnatural demeanor, or of a heedlessness that only too clearly betrays a lack of awareness of what they are about, as though they were simply moving from one part of the church to another.

We do not come to church to "attend the service," which usually means as a spectator, but in order, along with the priest, to serve God. Everything we do: our entering, being present, our kneeling and sitting and standing, our reception of the sacred nourishment, should be divine service. This is when all we do "overflows" from the awareness of a collected heart and the mind's attentiveness.

Such composure is all the more necessary since liturgical action is devoid of what otherwise enforces attention: namely, utility. When I seat myself at my desk and pick up a manuscript, my attention naturally passes to it; when I do a job in my workshop, I unconsciously pull myself together, otherwise it will miscarry. Everywhere some utilitarian purpose to be accomplished binds my attention. In the Mass there are no such "purposes." The believer simply steps into the presence of his God and remains there for him. The liturgy is a thing of exalted "purposelessness," but it is filled with the sense of sacred serving, and over it reigns the sublimity of God. Here composure means everything. Hence it must be willed and practiced. Otherwise our "service" grows dull, indolent, and careless—an insult to divine Majesty.

6. COMPOSURE AND PARTICIPATION

U ntil now our attention has been directed mainly to the liturgical
word. But Holy Mass does not consist only, even primarily, of words,
though the liturgy does include forms of divine service of which this is
true: vespers or choral prayer, generally. The Mass, on the other hand, is
fundamentally an act. The words the Lord used to establish it do not run:
"Say this in memory of me" or "Consider, proclaim, praise what has taken
place," but "Do." True, the Mass begins as an oral service and stretches as
such from the preparation at the foot of the altar to the *Credo*, and it re-
sumes this nature toward the end, from the Communion to the last Gospel.
Between the two parts comes action: the gift-offerings are prepared; the
mystery of the transubstantiation is executed; the sacred nourishment is
proffered and received. Thus the believer's task consists not only in hearing
and speaking the text of the Mass but also in taking part in the sacred act,
and once again the prerequisite of participation is inner composure.

Today it is not easy to speak of genuine participation. This is due
largely to the development that the liturgy of the Lord's memorial has
undergone. The first congregation was the group of disciples at table. This
original form of community at the table continued for a short time, as long
as the congregations were very small. The Acts of the Apostles describe
them: "And continuing daily with one accord in the temple, and breaking
bread in their houses, they took their food with gladness and simplicity

of heart, praising God and being in favor with all the people. And day by day the Lord added to their company such as were to be saved" (Acts 2:46–47). Here all still participated directly in the execution of the sacred act: they sat together at the table over the Divine Supper. We get the same picture from the first Epistle to the Corinthians (10:15–17; 11:17–34). Then, however, the congregations began to grow, and their numbers forced a new form on the sacred action. It lost its original, immediate character, and became stylized, transposed to the plane of the liturgical-sacramental. In place of the realistic act we now have its symbolical representation. Table became altar, and thereby lost something of its direct associations. A large number of people were less able to participate than a smaller number, and involuntarily the believers' attitudes, shifted to that of a mere observers. The whole became more and more sharply divided into two parts: here the altar on which the sacred act is ritually executed; there the people, aware that they are represented by the priest, but no longer actually seated at the table. As time went on and the rooms for divine service became larger, the more consistently the new form took over; today little remains of the original form—strictly speaking, only the collection after the Offertory and the communion rail.

Certain details of the early form of the Mass could undoubtedly be restored. The liturgical movement has achieved much, but much still remains to be done. First of all, without innovations and artificialities, the Offertory could be developed so that its original sense is thrown into sharper relief and the congregation could participate in it more fully. In general, however, historical development cannot be turned back. As long as congregations have the size they must have at present, the possibility of direct participation will necessarily remain limited. It is up to us to see to it that participation does not consist only of these outward details.

To participate means to share in the task of another. Here that other is the priest. He is not there for himself but for the congregation. By means of the words he speaks and gestures he makes in the power of his office, something happens—through Christ. Everyone present is called upon to share in that happening. The priest responds to it, not privately for himself, but for all. And again all are invited to share in his invocation, celebration, adoration, pleading, and thanksgiving. The celebrant's actions radiate in all directions far beyond his personal life. This is so primarily that all may and should enter into them.

How does such entry take place? First of all, through the participants' vital awareness of what is happening.

When the Offertory prayer is spoken and the priest uncovers the chalice, we should say to ourselves: "Now the gift-offerings with which the mystery will be celebrated are being prepared. What the Lord instructed his disciples to do when he told them to prepare for the Feast of the Passover, and what the first congregations did when each believer stepped forward with his offering of bread, wine, oil, is being done—now." Today all the preparations have been telescoped to the brief movements with which the priest lifts up the paten with the host and replaces it, receives the wine from the server, pours and mixes it with water, raises the chalice and puts it down again.[5]

Here we must realize that these few gifts on the altar stand for all that was formerly given and done in preparation for the Lord's Supper, and for the needs of the poor brothers and sisters in Christ; whatever is done for the least of these is done "for me." Something else belongs with the bread and wine: the money-offering of the faithful. I hesitate to add this, particularly in view of the often undignified manner in which the "jingle-bag" makes the rounds or coins clank into the box. Surely this matter could be managed differently; it should be, for the money represents the abundant, personal gifts once brought to the altar—a poor representative, to be sure! How much more alive this act was when one brought bread from his own oven, another jug of wine, a third jar of oil. Those offerings had a form and speech of their own. Now we have only cold coin. But we should neither lament what is past nor dream of future impossibilities; money is the modern substitute for goods. Hence our participation in the offering demands that this impoverished gesture be made as well as possible. We must not, for example, start fishing for our gift in church, breaking thereby the quiet of the ceremony. We should thoughtfully prepare our gift at home, and not in the spirit with which we respond to an irksome if not presumptuous demand, but in the spirit of a genuine "offering," a sacrifice that we really feel. And when we place the money in the basket, let it be with reverence to God and with charity to all.

When the *Sanctus* has been spoken and the Canon of the Mass begins, we should remind ourselves: "Now I shall witness, indeed partake in, what the ancient Church called *actio*—the essential act." We must give it our full attention. As soon as silence reigns again[6] we should say to ourselves: "The Lord's last will and testament is being executed. He said: 'As often as you shall do these things, in memory of me shall you do them.'" What happened in the room of the Last Supper is taking place here: Christ comes. He is present in his salutary love and in the destiny which it met. The priest acts, but we must act with him by being inwardly present, by watching him every moment at the altar table, identifying ourselves with his every gesture. (Thus I bring myself to a profound consciousness of what is taking place, a consciousness that can overflow into action: I can personally approach and receive the sacred food.)

Then comes the *Agnus Dei*. The priest says the prayer of preparation for Communion and partakes of the sacred food. He then shows the faithful the host saying: "Behold the Lamb of God, behold him who takes away the sins of the world." And he gives it to those at the communion rail. Thus another of the Lord's commands: "Take you all and eat this" is obeyed. Alas, not as frequently as it might. Often the act itself is left out, and participation consists only in thinking and visualizing, attending, willing and loving, watching and sharing. But this too is good and great, for the act of the spirit is as important—or more important—than movements of hands and feet. The priest acts and we act with him, following observantly, spiritually. Naturally, we must be genuinely active, not simply watchful. We must overcome the unconcern, sleepiness, indolence, and inertia which keep us from the sacred act so that we may enter into it vitally.

Composure alone enables us to do this. When the mind is not collected and the heart is restless and inattentive, the believer will be occasionally conscious of a word or gesture, or the bell will remind him that one of the high points of the Mass is at hand; never will he be in that state of active, watchful vitality which alone permits genuine participation. Liturgical action begins with learning composure. Everything else: the use of the missal, instruction on the meaning and history of the Mass, and the chorale are important and fruitful—as long as they are rooted in self-collectedness.

Composure and the participation springing from it must be practiced. There is a much-aired opinion that only the prayer and religious act rising involuntarily from within are genuine. This is erroneous. Prayer and religious action are life. But life consists only partly in spontaneous acts; most of life is service and conscious effort, both at least as important as impulsive activity. We so often use the phrase "church service." Why don't we for once take it seriously? Service does not imply action overflowing naturally from an inner need, but rather action performed in obedience at the appointed time. When it is service in God's sight rather than man's, it is not only external but also—and preeminently—inner action and participation. Hence divine serving must be learned, practiced over and over again so it may become increasingly vigilant, profound, and true. Then we shall be granted also that living experience which is beyond all willing and practicing. We shall be seized and so drawn into the act of salvation that we really exist in the memorial of the Lord, a work not of men, but of God. It is the imperishable reality of the salutary act God sent in the hour of the sacred ceremony which enters the world and time ever and again. Consciousness of this divine event is doubtless the greatest gift the Mass can give. It comes, however, only when God gives it. Our task lies in the effort and loyalty of service.[7]

---

7. THE HOLY PLACE

The Mass is celebrated in church, in a holy place. Under special conditions it may be celebrated elsewhere: in the open air when some great event has attracted great masses of people; on shipboard; even, at times of stress, in a private home. The celebration of Mass on such occasions can be very impressive: festive and imposing, gravely suggestive of God's providence and man's destiny, or intimately protective in the presence of danger. Still, such celebrations are always exceptional. Normally, the Mass belongs in its own particular place in the sacred room of the church.

The standard objection to this is so trite that it can no longer be taken seriously: God can be served anywhere and "experienced" anywhere. Probably the speaker will bring up the Bible passage about the quiet chamber or insist that the just man is particularly close to God in nature and that one can be more aware of him while bending over a flower than in a stuffy church. There is a good deal to be said in reply to this. For one thing, it might be asked, how much of it is genuine objection and how much pious talk? Does the speaker really practice intimate conversation with God in that quiet chamber of his? Does he really commune with him in the woods and before a rose? More important is the latent criticism behind the objections: the Church mistrusts men's piety and declares nature evil; therefore, with priestly hostility to life, she shuts off an artificial area in which she celebrates a ritual that has nothing in common with genuine men or with the uncorrupted freshness of nature. The criticism is remarkable, particularly since the same Church is blamed for not taking religion "spiritually" or "purely" enough, for allowing her ceremonies to slip back into the natural, and for practicing "a Christianity that is fundamentally little more than a veiled paganism." It seems that the Church is accused of all possible shortcomings, with the result—truth's mysterious self-justification—that one objection cancels the other.

Actually, the Church takes the world very seriously. She knows that everything is created by God, sustained by his power, and filled with his meaning. But she also knows that the world is full of enchanting power, and that it incessantly attempts to draw men from the Creator to the created: to itself. Hence, in spite of her knowledge that all things belong to God, and of her desire to return them to him from whom they came, the Church sets aside a place that has been severed from all other connections and purposes in order to belong to him in a very special way. Here man is meant to become aware of something different both from nature and from human works: of the holy.

By holiness we do not mean that soaring sense of mystery that can make itself felt anywhere—under a heaven full of stars, in a forest, or in the presence of some great human tragedy or fulfillment. We use the word in the strict sense of revelation: God alone is holy. Holiness is his essential characteristic. It means that he is pure, terribly and gloriously pure; that he does not merely repel evil, but hates and judges it; that he is the fullness of all good, is himself the good, and all other good is merely a reflection of him; that he lives in an unapproachable mystery which knows no intimacy, yet is the goal of man's unconditional and deepest longing. If we wish to learn what God's holiness is, we must consult not the poets but the prophets.

How then can a place be holy? Not of itself. No created thing is capable by its own nature of furnishing a dwelling-place for God's holiness. A place becomes holy only when God himself has sanctified it. This happens—and now we touch the heart of our problem—through God's visiting that place and establishing it as his residence.

But God is omnipresent—in heaven, on earth, everywhere! Yes, God fills all things, governs all things, and sustains all things in such a way that he is not in any particular place, but that every place is in him. That is true. Everything is necessarily and irrevocably in God because it has been created by him. In his speech before the Areopagus, St. Paul says: "For in him we live and move and have our being" (Acts 17:28). Not a grain of the world's dust could exist were it not sustained by God. Nevertheless, a real divine presence, divine "inhabiting" does exist. The Old Testament is the story of God's coming and being with men, of his guiding and ruling them and of the fate which his love thereby took upon itself. However, God's essential, supreme act of concern—of cohabitation with men—is Christ. St. John opens his gospel by saying:

> He was in the world,
> and the world was made through him,
> and the world knew him not.
> He came unto his own,
> and his own received him not . . .
> And the Word was made flesh.
> and dwelt among us. (Jn 1:10–11,14)

Where Jesus was, God was. When Jesus entered a temple or house, or walked down a street, God was present in that particular place in a special way. Indeed, in the manner in which he was there, he was not simultaneously outside the temple, in another street, or in someone else's house. It sounds odd to speak like this, childish and primitive; nevertheless, it is pure truth. Truth is always truth; it means that something real and essential becomes so apparent that it is observed and expressed. But truth exists on different levels, each with its own rank, one higher and nobler than another. That God is everywhere, that he rules every part of the world as its Creator, sustaining it with his power and love, is a wonderful truth; but a much higher and holier truth reveals to us that in Christ God came specifically so that where Christ visited, God was present in a new and particular manner, which our mind cannot comprehend because it is unable to reconcile it to the idea of divine omnipresence but which the vital depths of our spirit accept as the supreme mystery of divine love.

Here are the reasons for the Church's being the "house of God" and "holy." First, because the bishop by the power of his office has freed her from the usual bonds with the world of men and nature, from the uses and ends of daily existence, and dedicated her to God. Thus she becomes his own, an expression of his divine reserve, an image of his holiness, and a reminder of his power. But this is only preparatory. In the deepest sense of the word, she is sanctified through the celebration of the Lord's memorial. By transubstantiation he himself "descends" and is present in a unique form. With his all-rescuing love and the essence of his salutary death, he stops for a time in the midst of the congregation. In Communion he offers himself as food and drink; then he departs. Again and again it happens—the "Passover of the Lord." Church is the room in which this coming, lingering, and departure occur. If we are anxious to collect ourselves and to overcome inertia, we would do well to remember that this is the holy place that he is about to enter.

8. THE ALTAR: THRESHOLD

We have just distinguished between God's special presence in his own house and his all-sustaining omnipresence in the world he created. We also replied to the current objection that man can experience God equally well everywhere. Of course, this is possible, as it is also possible to experience everywhere the illusion of false Christianity more readily than genuine contact with the Creator of the world. Moreover, there is always the disquieting suspicion that those who insist on their encounters with God in woods and cowers do not have in mind the God of revelation, but a vague, pantheistic "Mother Nature" or mysterious "Life Force," or whatever else these questionable varieties of "religious experience" are called. The real God has no resemblance with the "God" such experiences presuppose. He speaks in the plain, exact words of his messengers through the person, life, and death of Jesus Christ. He challenges the world, arousing it from its captivity, demanding that it recognize the truth and be converted. The otherness of that conversion is stressed by the fact that the celebration of God's mystery does *not* take place just anywhere: neither in the spaciousness of nature, nor in the intimacy of a home, but in the unique, clearly circumscribed area of the church. Thus we find the constantly repeated procedure: the believer goes to the house of God, crosses the threshold, and enters the sacred room within. This is an important part of genuine piety. He remains "present," listens, speaks, acts, and serves. Then he leaves, returns to the world of men or to the private realm of his home, taking with him what he has experienced as instruction, guidance, and strength.

There is also a special order established within the sacred interior. It is essential to the liturgy that the important acts of which it is composed are not left to chance or to the momentary spiritual situation but are arranged and specified with the greatest care. The Lord's memorial sacrifice cannot take place anywhere in the church but only at one particular spot—the altar.

The altar is a great mystery. Its religious archetype is to be found in almost all faiths; indeed, I doubt that it is fundamentally absent from any. It appears in the Old Testament. Precise laws determine how it is to be fashioned, cared for, and served. In the New Testament it is not actually discussed; but we do encounter it, for example, in the visions of the apocalypse. When the books of the New Testament were being written, the altar was the table at which the congregation celebrated the Sacred Supper. Very soon, however, it began to take on its own characteristics, and in the catacombs we find it in its earliest form. What then is the altar? Its meaning is probably most clearly suggested by two images: it is threshold, and it is table.

Threshold is door, and it has a double significance: border and crossing over. It indicates where one thing ends and another begins. The border, which marks the end of the old, makes possible entry into the new. As a threshold, the altar creates first the border between the realm of the world and the realm of God. The altar reminds us of the remoteness in which he lives "beyond the altar," as we might say, meaning divine distance; or "above the altar," meaning divine loftiness—both to be understood of course not spatially but spiritually. They mean that God is the Intangible One, far removed from all approaching, from all grasping; that he is the all-powerful, Majestic One immeasurably exalted above earthly things and earthly striving. Such breadth and height are founded not on measure, but on God's essence: his holiness to which man of himself has no access.

On the other hand, this is not to be understood merely spiritually, or rather, merely intellectually. In the liturgy everything is symbolical. But symbol is more than a corporeal form representing something incorporeal. Let us take, for example, a representation of Justice: a woman, blindfolded, and holding scales in her hands. Such justice is not apparent. First one must be instructed that the bandaged eyes mean that a judge is no respecter of persons; the scales, that to each is to be measured out his exact due. This is an allegory whose meaning is not directly perceived.

The liturgy also contains allegories; but its basic forms are symbols. The meaning is actually hidden, yet it reveals itself in a particular thing or person, much as the human soul, itself invisible, becomes perceptible and approachable in the expression and movements of a face. So is it in the Church. The altar is not an allegory but a symbol. The thoughtful believer does not have to be taught that it is a border, that "above it" stretch inaccessible heights and "beyond it" the reaches of divine remoteness; somehow he becomes aware of this.

To grasp the mystery all that is necessary on the part of the believer is intrinsic readiness and calm reflection; then his heart will respond with reverence. In a vital hour he may even have an experience somewhat similar to that of Moses when he guarded his flocks in the loneliness of Mount Horeb. Suddenly "The Lord appeared to him in a flame of fire out of the midst of a bush: and he saw that the bush was on fire and was not burnt. And Moses said: 'I will go and see this great sight, why the bush is not burnt.' And when the Lord saw that he went forward to see, he called to him out of the midst of the bush, and said: 'Moses, Moses.' And he answered: 'Here I am.' And he said: 'Come not nigh hither. Put off the shoes from thy feet: for the place whereon thou standest is holy ground'" (Ex 3:2–5).

It is essential for every one of us to experience at some time or another the fear of the Lord, to be repelled by him from the sacred place, that we may know with all our being that God is God, and we are but man. Trust in God, nearness to him and security in him remain thin and feeble when personal knowledge of God's exclusive majesty and awful sanctity do not counterbalance them. We do well to pray to God for this experience, and the place where it is most likely to be granted us is before his altar.

Threshold is not, however, only borderline; it is also crossing over. One can step over it into the adjacent room, or standing on it, receive him who comes from the other side. It is something that unites, a place of contact and encounter. This too is contained in the symbol of the altar. The essence of revelation is the news that God loves us. God's love is not simply the love which we find also in ourselves, infinitely intensified. Inconceivable mystery, it had to be revealed: an unheard-of act that we can begin to fathom only when it is clear to us who God is and who we are. Its real expression is to be found in the tremendous event of the Incarnation, when God abandoned his sacred reserve, came to us, and became one of us, sharing with us human life and human destiny. Now he is with us, "on our side." Such is his love, and it creates a nearness that man alone never could have conceived. All this is expressed by the altar. It reminds us that God turns to us; from his heights he steps down to us; out of his remoteness he approaches us. The altar is the sign of God's presence among us, in us. And the same altar suggests further that there is a way leading us, remote, isolated creatures that we are, back to our Creator; from the depths of our sin "up" to his holiness; that we can follow it—to be sure, not on our own strength, but on that which his grace supplies. We can cross the border only because God crossed it to come to us. His descent draws us upward. He himself, the One Who Has Come, *is* "the way, and the truth, and the life."

Knowledge of the possibility of passing above and beyond is a primordial Christian experience which most intimately affects man's relations to God—a passing that is not simple continuation along a known route, but a traversing of certain limits. The realms that it separates are different; between them stands a door which can open and also close. We are enabled to make the passage by hope, which declares it possible (but only when we heed an innate reticence, which cautions that it is never self-understood). The instant hope becomes importunity or trust presumption, the instant the sacred security of grace lapses into habit, the door closes, and most firmly when its existence has been entirely forgotten and the believer innocently assumes that all is as it should be. At this point too we would do well to ask that we may realize vividly that we are "children" of "the Father's house," yet must stand "in fear and trembling."

Threshold really lies everywhere in the simple fact that God is Creator and man creature; this fact is heightened by man's sinfulness, which makes him unable to stand before the Holy God. Yet God has stooped to us in an act of saving love and laid out for us the road to himself. Thus everywhere we are confronted by sacred barriers repelling us but also by the possibility of their opening for us. What we call prayer is the mysterious process of that opening.

Every time we invoke God, we approach his threshold and pass over it. In the altar the barrier presents itself in a form symbolizing God's revelation, for there in the mystery of the Mass it comes to its own in a very special way. Through Christ's self-sacrifice in salutary death, a sacrifice which presupposed the Incarnation of God's Son, the altar-threshold appears most clearly as the borderline which shows who Holy God is and what our sin. But the altar-threshold is also the crossing-over *par excellence*, because God became man so that we might become "partakers of the divine nature." The altar is indeed the "holy place" before which we can say as we can nowhere else: "I am here, O Lord."

9. The Altar: Table

The altar is the threshold to God's immanence. Through Christ, God ceased to be the Unknown, the Inaccessible One; he turned to us, came to us, and became one of us in order that we might go to him and become one with him. The altar is the frontier, the border where God comes to us and we go to him in a most special manner.

At this point a few remarks about the images used to express sacred mysteries are in order. The images unlock the storehouse of God's riches, and they help us to concentrate on particular aspects of divine reality with all our power. When we consider the altar as a threshold, we see one particular trait, leaving out of consideration any other, such as that expressed by the concept "table." The images used are necessarily taken from objects of our own experience. But, since we are not cut off from God and his life as is one room in a house from another, we must not put too much emphasis on the inability of images adequately to express divine realities. If we do, we lose something precious, something essential. Images are not makeshifts handy for children and the vulgar crowd, which the cultured elite, wrestling with "pure" concepts, should despise. When Jacob, Abraham's grandson, woke from his great dream, he cried: "How terrible is this place! This is no other but the house of God, and the gate of heaven" (Gn 28:17). And St. John writes: "and behold, a door standing open in heaven, and the former voice, which I had heard as of a trumpet speaking with me, said, 'come up hither, and I will show thee the things that must come to pass hereafter'" (Rv 4:1). Now if we were to say that "door" is here only a figure of speech suggesting that God is invisible yet near, that no one can reach him, but that he can draw us to himself, we would be correct but we would fail to grasp the basic meaning of St. John's words. St. John wrote "door" because he meant door—and not only poetically. The intellect may attempt to express in concepts and sentences all that the image "door" implies; but such concepts are mere props to the essential, not more. The truth is the other way around: it is the image that is the reality; the mind can only attempt to plumb it. The image is richer than the thought; hence the act by which we comprehend an image, gazing, is richer, more profound, vital, and storied than the thought. People today are, if the word may be permitted, over-conceptualistic. We have lost the art of reading images and parables, of enacting symbols. We could relearn some of this by encouraging and practicing the power of vision, a power which has been neglected for too long.

But to return to our subject, the mystery of the altar is only partially suggested by the image of the threshold; altar is also table.

The presentiment of a sacred table at which not only man but also divinity takes its place is to be found in the religions of all peoples. Everywhere the pious believer places gifts upon an altar so that the godhead may accept them. The idea that these gifts belong to the godhead and no longer to men is conveyed by their destruction or withdrawal from human use. The body of the sacrificial animal is burned and the drink poured out upon the ground. This immolation symbolizes what is contained in the process of death: the "passing over" to the other side—the realm of the divine. A second process is often related to the first. Not everything is "given over"; part is retained—or rather returned, for what was destroyed represented the whole—now to be enjoyed by the offerers. Thus godhead and man are nourished by the same sacred food. Indeed, behind this concept lies one still more profound: man's offering stands for himself, is really himself;

the true offering is human sacrifice. Again, the offering stands for the godhead itself; true nourishment is divine life. From a certain standpoint these conceptions are very profound, though closer examination reveals that they have sunk into gloom, worldliness, and animalism. The godhead, then, lives from the life of man of a tribe, a people; on the other hand, man sees in his godhead the spiritual mainspring of his own life and that of his clan, tribe, people. Divinity has need of man and man of divinity, for in the final analysis they are the same; sacrifice is the constantly renewed process of this union.

Such conceptions are totally absent from the Old Testament. The God to whose altar offerings are brought is neither the vital principle of a people nor the secret of the world's vitality, but Creator and Lord of all that is. The offering is an acknowledgment of his lordship; it in no way affects his potency but recognizes that all things are his and that man may dispose of them only with his permission. Strictly speaking, the animal from the flock should be slaughtered only before the altar, not because God has any need of its blood but because all life is his property; the harvest should be consumed only before the altar, since everything that bears its seed "within itself" belongs to God. This idea is expressed in the sacrifice of livestock and in the offering of the fields' first fruits. Only then does man receive herd and harvest back from the altar for his own use.

The altar is the table to which the heavenly Father invites us. Through salvation we have become sons and daughters of God, and his house is ours. At the altar we enjoy the intimate community of his sacred table. From his hand we receive the "bread of heaven," the word of truth, and, far excelling all imaginable gifts, his own incarnate Son, the living Christ (see Jn 6). What is given us, then, is at once corporeal reality and sentient truth: Life and Person, in short—Gift.

But if we ask whether at the sacred table God too receives something, whether the age-old presentiment of a real community of table between God and man is not also fulfilled in the clean air of Christian faith, the answer is not easy. Fear of being irreverent makes us cautious. However, we can point to a mystery that fills the letters of St. Paul and appears also in the farewell speeches of St. John's gospel. The fruit of the divine sojourn on earth is salvation. This means not only our forgiveness and justification but also that the world is "brought home" to the Father. And again not only in the sense that we return to God in love and obedience but that men—and through men the world in all its reality—is received into divine life. God desires this. When we are told that he loves us, this does not mean that he is merely benevolent toward us; the word *love* is meant in all its abundance.

God longs for men. He wants to have his creatures close to him. When Christ cried from the cross, "I thirst," a dying man's bodily torment was indeed expressed, but much more besides (Jn 19:28). Similarly at Jacob's well, when the disciples encouraged Jesus to eat the food they had brought, he replied: "My food is to do the will of him who sent me, to accomplish his work" (Jn 4:34). This is mysterious hungering and thirsting—the hunger and thirst of God! St. Augustine writes that the receiving of the Eucharist does not mean so much that we partake of the divine life offered us, as that divine life draws us into itself. These thoughts should not be pressed too far, for they are holy. It is important, however, to know that a mystery of divine-human love and communion does exist and that it is realized at the altar.

10. Holy Day

The holy place, set apart from the rest of the world, came into being when God's Son appeared on earth: when he was conceived in Nazareth, born in Bethlehem, and lived among us in Palestine—and in such a manner that it could be said: "There he is; there he goes." Is there perhaps a holy time as well?

Again it is a question of a time not of man's making. There exists no deed, no experience, no dedication by which man of himself can so sanctify a day or an hour that it becomes holy in God's sight. God alone can sanctify a period of time by personally entering into it. I am "in time" because I live and unfold in time, act in it, experience destiny; but are such things conceivable of God? Our answer is spontaneous; it is "No." God lives not only forever, but eternally; his life has nothing to do with time. He neither grows nor declines, develops nor changes—all that would involve time— but realizes his infinite essence wholly and perfectly in purest actuality. He did create time, as he created everything else that exists; more correctly, he created the world, which exists in time. Thus he is present in all time, in its smallest as in its largest fraction: in the day, hour, minute—in the infinitesimally brief flashes known to physicists, as well as in years, centuries, millennia and those no longer conceivable masses of time in which astronomers reckon. God fills them all, and no one period is holier than another. What is decisive is whether the universally governing sanctity of God is able to step to the fore in a specific instance, moving men and engraving itself into the historical memory.

We are not concerned here with the problem just stated. Such a "holy hour" could appear at any time: in the evolution of nature, in the relations between members of a family, or in history. When the liturgy speaks of sacred time it means something specific, similar to the specificity of the sacred place. What it is, however, only revelation can say. And it does say, with all clarity: one of the seven days of the week is sacred to God, the day on which he "rested" after creating the universe.

The message given to us by revelation is meant to be taken realistically. It signifies something mysterious, yes, but also something explicit. In the book of Genesis God's handiwork is described as being completed in the course of a week. Six days long God creates and on the seventh he rests. The biblical report has nothing to do with the question: when, in what period, did the stars, plants, and animals come into existence? "Week" does not signify a period of time in the ordinary sense of the word; it is rather a symbol for the wise, humanly intelligible order in which creation took place. But over and above this, the word "week" means something very precise: from the earliest beginnings of the world God arranged its seven days in such a fashion as to allow man six for his work; the seventh, however, he reserved for himself, setting it apart because "on this day," having completed creation, he entered into his rest.

The holiness of the Sabbath does not stem, then, from man's repose. It is not a natural part of the rhythm of life: the idea, for instance, that man is bound, oppressed by his duties and objectives for six days and that on the seventh he is free to devote himself to holy acts. This is also true; in the rhythm of work and relaxation a mystery of religious repose really can be experienced. But what faith and the liturgy have in mind is something quite different: the sacredness of the Lord's Day is due not to any experience of man, however holy, but to God and to his resting on that day. Or to put it more precisely, there exists for God in connection with creation a mystery known as "divine repose." We cannot understand it—what could it possibly mean, rest for the Omnipotent? When we accept this mystery on faith, however, we do sense the presence of something very profound. God is not only the eternal Spirit who is spoken of in philosophical absolutes; he is also the Acting One, of whom it may be said that he decides, that he rises, creates, forms, arranges, and that he rests (see Gn 2:2).

It is this mystery of God's rest which permeates the seventh day of the week, as the others are permeated by the mystery of divine activity.

The whole week is a mystery; in fact, all time is. Not essentially, in itself; not through human life, but through divine creativeness. Hence it is a mystery which cannot be plumbed by geological or anthropological research. It can only be known through revelation.[8]

Sunday has an almost sacramental character. In the sacrament, a natural process, like that of bathing or of confessing one's guilt is related to the governing of grace. During the natural act, supernatural grace becomes effective, much as the movements of the soul activate the body. Something similar is to be found in the mystery of the Sabbath.

The natural tension caused by six days of work and its slackening on the day of rest create the form into which God has sunk the mystery of his repose in order to convey it to us. To keep the Sabbath is to become aware of the mystery of divine rest, to revere it, and to express it in our arrangement of the day.

The thought is as beautiful as its realization is difficult. If discussed at all, it should not be distorted by daydreams but should be considered realistically.

Precisely because Sunday is not a product of the natural life rhythm, it is vulnerable. The merely natural somehow manages to assert itself; the roots of Sunday, however, lie in revelation. Thus it is easily destroyed, in spite of the important natural need which it also meets. Other considerations—economic, social, or what have you—constantly shove it aside. Work gnaws at it; amusement elbows its way into it, crowding out holiness;

the significance of "keeping holy" is itself misunderstood and rest is imposed with a resultant boredom that is worse than if work had continued. Thus Sunday poses a real problem, which each of us must solve according to his own particular circumstances.

The day is important for the individual, but above all for the family. We must understand what is at stake, realize its value for us, and tackle the problem as energetically and wholeheartedly as we do other matters important to us.

One more point. From the liturgy it is clear that the day does not begin with the morning, nor with midnight, but on the evening before with the vigil. There is a profound insight in this. It is not a question of the astronomical but of the living day. The one is a mathematically exact fraction of time, which begins with a certain second, regardless of what takes place in it; whereas the other, living day, is a continuously renewed life-form. Then when does it begin? We could say at the moment of our deepest sleep, when life is at its stillest, on condition that our sleep itself begins and moves and ends properly. Then the day would stretch from this moment to a corresponding moment in the following night. That moment is unknown. We do not "accomplish" sleep; it is something that happens to us. Hence we must place the beginning we sought somewhere before the moment of falling asleep. Sleep is profoundly influenced by the hours that immediately precede it; therefore the problem of Sunday begins on Saturday evening, and it is up to each of us to see how we can meet its sacred challenge.

11. Holy Day and Holy Hour

So the heavens and the earth were finished, and all the furniture of them. And on the seventh day God ended his work which he had made; and he rested on the seventh day from all his work which he had done. And he blessed the seventh day, and sanctified it: because in it he had rested from all his work which God created and made" (Gn 2:1–3). The seventh day, the Sabbath, the holy day of the New Testament, however, is Sunday, the first day of the week. Here again something typical of the New Testament has occurred. Jesus Christ was not only the Executant of the Old Testament but its Lord as well. In him the promise of the coming Messiah, which gleams throughout the Old Testament, is fulfilled. All the former things moved toward him—their Perfector; he gave them a new significance and brought them to a close so conclusive that their representatives regarded him as an enemy of God and killed him, an act which but executed the institution of his redeeming love. With Christ's death and Resurrection the new order began. The evening before his death, while establishing the Eucharist, Jesus spoke with divine simplicity of the "new covenant in my blood" (Lk 22:20). The day of Easter on which he rose again, crowning his mission, now becomes the new day of completion. Again God "rests" from his work of creation—this time the creation from which the new man, the new heaven and earth are supposed to emerge. This day returns every week as Sunday, memorial of the first creation's wedding with the

45

second. The divine repose of the Sabbath now mingles with the triumph of the Resurrection. Into the hum of peace breaks the fanfare of victory. Promise and fulfillment have become one! For the Sabbath looked back— in eternity—to the beginning. Sunday looks forward—in eternity—to the end, to what is to come. It has an eschatological character. It proclaims Christ's new creation, the new world born of his deed and one day to be revealed in eternity.

We asked whether it is possible to speak of God's resting, since he is "He who is" the Omnipotent One, eternal and unchanging; revelation replies that he truly makes decisions, creates, and rests from creating. This double aspect of the all-pervasive, all-governing God who is yet personally free to come and go and act in a specific instance is proclaimed throughout Scripture. The Bible recounts his selection of a particular person, his sealing a covenant of loyalty with him, his consolidation of that covenant with the nation which grew from the chosen man's descendants, his divine guidance and support in their constant struggles against their own inertia and stubbornness, his never-failing loyalty, and his rescuing them from repeated apostasy.

Again and again God experiences the lot of magnanimity betrayed. The account goes on to tell how he then revealed himself in all his reality: the Father sends his eternal Son into the world as the long-awaited Messiah. The Holy Spirit governs that entire life, and everyone is aware of its unheard-of power. Finally, God's Son, accepting with supreme readiness the fate prepared for him among men, allows the storm clouds of centuries-old opposition to the divine to gather, break over his head, and slay him. The completion of this act on Calvary, the victory of the Resurrection, is expressed in the day of the Lord.

But God's lot among men finds another expression in time, namely, in the Mass itself.

The *Gottesschicksal*, or divine fate, took place in time. As divine act and fate, however, it issued from the divine will. It took place once as an earthly event with beginning and end. Simultaneously it is an unchanging reality in eternity. There Christ stands with his passion and death before the Father. Before he died he willed that this salutary fulfillment be constantly remembered. At the Last Supper he gave his friends the bread of his body and the wine of his blood, exhorting them to "do this" in his memory. As often as those authorized to do so obey this command, what occurred then occurs again—in the present. The "memorial" is no mere recollection; it is a return to actual being. Through the act of the Lord's memorial the eternal reality of God's earthly destiny, renewed ever and again, steps into time. This entry is the holy hour, the constantly recurring "now." It is not as though there existed one hour that man reserved for his God; God himself, bearing his salutary destiny, enters into the hour, which attains self-realization through him. It now becomes part of the new creation. Through such an hour time contains eternity, and eternity embraces time.

When the eternal God took upon himself our human transitoriness, *sacred time* in the real sense of the words came into being. At first that was the time that lay between the angel's annunciation and the Lord's departure. Within those years the incarnate Son of God lived, worked, and suffered among us then and only then. During the reign of Caesar Augustus, God really became man, and while Pontius Pilate was procurator of Judea he really died, not sooner, not later. Between those two events the eternal *Logos* existed as a man. This earthly sojourn is renewed in the Mass. When the priest, empowered by the Lord himself, speaks the words over the bread and the wine, Christ walks alive and real among his congregation until he gives himself as nourishment in the Sacred Supper. Again a definite span of time with beginning and end—the "Passover of the Lord" in the most literal sense of the phrase.

To participate properly in the Mass it is essential that we be aware of its temporalness: of its beginning, continuation, and end. This brief portion of time enfolds eternity. Customs like that of exposing the Blessed Sacrament during the Mass are inclined to obscure this. They are a concession to the congregation's desire to have the Lord present in the mystery of the Eucharist as openly, as intimately, and as long as possible. There is something very vital in this desire and in the Church's response to it. Upon closer examination, however, we notice that the privilege is not granted without specific limitations. All too easily the exposition of the Blessed Sacrament can blur the sense of sacred temporalness in the Mass. The constant figure of the host, star-like above the altar, cancels the sense of the Lord's coming, pausing, and departing.

It is very important to experience the passover of the sacred moment emerging from eternity. It catches us up into itself, and while it lasts we are different from what we are at all other times. Then it dismisses us, and we fall back into the transitoriness of day-to-day existence. But if we have vitally participated in it, we take with us the seed of that holy eternity that comes from the Resurrection, and our life in the transitory world is changed.

12. THE SACRED ACT

Following our discussion of the sacred order of time and space, it would now be interesting to turn to that which takes place in them: the act of the Mass itself. But since we are going to consider the Mass in detail in Part Two of this book, only one aspect of it need be mentioned here: the nature of its action.

A religious act can have various origins. What we desire most today is immediate experience. Let us suppose that a group of people has just been rescued from mortal danger. It is not difficult to imagine that in response to some inner urge they grow still, remove their hats, or make some other earnest gesture of reverence and gratitude to God. Their act would be a direct expression of their experience, possible only at that moment and for those particular people. Were it to be repeated, it would at once become artificial and embarrassing.

The act could also spring from the consciousness of a significant, regularly recurring hour: for instance, after the labor, encounters, and providential experiences of the day, before man enters upon the darkness of sleep which heralds death's long night. At this moment his impulse is to pause, to collect and place himself in the hands of his Maker, and if he has learned to heed such inner promptings, he will do so. With the beginning of the day comes a similar impulse. Then too man is conscious of the need to do something religious, to become established in himself and turn to face what God expects of him during the coming day. At the close of the old year, the opening of the new, such an impulse, intensified, also makes itself felt. Acts of this kind are repeatable, even under varying circumstances and by different people; for they spring, not from a unique experience but from the recurrent rhythms of existence.

Finally, a religious act can also be instituted, that is, some act can be made valid and obligatory. Only he who possesses authority can institute with genuine validity. God did so during the Exodus from Egypt, when he commanded that the liberation be annually commemorated in the feast of the Passover. It was during this commemoration at the Last Supper that Christ instituted a second commemoration—that of his death. His oneness with the Father's will, his life and salutary destiny, and his living, messianic reality—all are expressed in the words spoken over the bread and wine and in the common partaking of the sacred food. And he instructed his followers to repeat it forever: "As often as you shall do these things, in memory of me shall you do them." This is institution *par excellence*: the core of Christian divine service. When God established the law of the Passover, he instructed the people to offer sacrifice on a certain day, celebrating together a feast commemorating their former liberation from Egypt. This act, which emerged from the humanly possible, received its real significance from divine direction. The act Christ instituted is different. He did not say: "On a certain day of the year you are to come together and share a meal in friendship. Then shall the eldest bless bread and wine and invoke my memory." Such an act would be similar to the Passover, issuing from the humanly possible; only the event it was celebrating would be divine. Christ spoke differently. His "do these things" implies "things I have just done"; yet what he did surpasses human possibility. It is an act of God springing as incomprehensibly from his love and omnipotence as the acts of Creation or the Incarnation. And such an act he entrusts to men! He does not say: "Pray God to do thus," but simply "do." Thus he places in human hands an act which can be fulfilled only by the divine. Its mystery is similar to that of sacred time and place, already discussed. Man acts; but in his human action is the act of God. And not only in the general sense that God is present in all human endeavor because all our reality, strength, wisdom, and will come from him. This is a specific, historical act; here the word "institution" has a special, unique significance. God determined, proclaimed, and instituted; man is to execute the act. When he does so, God makes of it something of which he alone is capable.

Subject to the divine nature of the act is a certain human attitude, a certain indispensable bearing. If something of the origin and freshness of the experience is to be transmitted, the individual must be aware of what is happening and have the vigor to express it. Its expression must be credible, vital, genuine, and powerful in word and gesture. If the act is to be related significantly to regularly returning hours or seasons, the participant must feel the truth of the relation and of the mystery behind it. He must have an expression for it that remains valid through all the variations of the hours. For the institutional act one other thing is necessary: not creative experience and repeatable expression, not the constantly renewed realization of its existential significance in our lives but obedience to the will of the Institutor. It is for men to "hear" the Lord and to do as he commands. It is service, as independent of personal experience as of comprehension of its natural significance. It is service in faith and obedience. It is not an independent human act, but acceptance of a divine undertaking that prepares a place for it, shapes for it a body of earthly cooperation. In the profoundest sense of the word it is a selfless act whereby man arrives at his true self. That is why the act of the Mass can be renewed time and again under the most varied circumstances of general as well as personal history, in hours of spiritual abundance and of spiritual need, in affliction and mourning or in freedom and joy.

13. The Revelatory Word

Holy Mass is an act; it is not, however, enacted mutely, but combines doing and speaking. It includes several varieties of words, and it is helpful not only to our understanding but also to our effective participation in the liturgy to realize this multiplicity and learn to distinguish between the different kinds of words employed.

First of all, there are the words from revelation. With them God tells man who he is and what the world is in his eyes; he proclaims his will and gives us his promise. They are Biblical words, and in the celebration of the Lord's memorial they confront us at every step. Indeed, the first part of the Mass consists almost entirely of speech; action is limited to the simplest movements, certain gestures and positions or the passing from one symbolical place to another.

Epistle and Gospel are readings taken directly from Scripture. The first, as the name suggests, from the letters of the apostles, but also from the Acts and from the Old Testament; the second, again indicated by the name, from the reports on the life of the Lord: the Gospels. The Biblical reading is continued in the sermon, which is intended to explain, enlarge upon, adopt, and apply the direct words of God. It loses its intrinsic character in the degree that it expresses instead the personal, human conceptions of the speaker.

God's word is a great mystery. Through it he himself speaks but in the speech of men. It appears that another form of communication also exists, a so-called "purely divine" form, in which God enlightens and directs the soul not through the medium of words but by a thought that stirs only from within, silent but immediately comprehended. Tidings of this kind can never be passed on to others; they apply solely to him who has received them. With revelation it is different. It is meant for all men at all times. Hence it takes the form in which the spiritual community of men asserts itself—that of the spoken word; like all speech, it is a purely human blend of idea and sound. God's wisdom has been placed in this human means of communication and can be removed and examined by itself at any time, but in such a way that his wisdom and the word containing it are an organic unit. Even the natural word cannot be separated from its audible sound and taken solely by itself, for it clings to its sound as the soul to the body. This unit now becomes, as it were, the body for a new "soul," the divine, much as a man already having body and soul is filled by grace, which makes of him a newer and higher being: the "new" or "spiritual" man described by St. Paul.

The divine words must be considered as whole words with shape and sound. To focus our attention only on the intelligible concept expressed by them would be folly; it would be rootless intellectual theory. A word is a wondrous reality: form and content, significance and love, intellect and heart, a full, round, vibrant whole. It is not barren information for us to consider and understand but a reality for us to encounter personally. We must receive and store it in all its earthiness, as well as its characteristic style and imagery. Then it proves its power. In the parable of the sower our Lord himself compares it to a seed in search of good ground. It possesses the power of growth, the strength to start and develop life. Hence we must not receive it as we grasp an idea with our minds but as earth receives a grain of wheat.

Revelation says that the world was created by the Word of God. God spoke: "Let there be . . ." By it we also were made, beings capable of hearing the word God gives us in revelation, summoning us to the new beginning and the new life of grace. Wherever we encounter his Word, we encounter God's creative power. To receive his Word means to step into the sphere of sacred possibility, where the new man, the new heaven, and the new earth are coming into being.

It is not sufficient merely to accept ideas and understand commandments. We must lay bare our hearts and minds to the power that comes to us from beyond.

God's Word is addressed not only to the intellect but to the whole man. (It has a human quality that seeks to become a living unit with mind and blood, soul and body.) Man, the entire man, must receive God's Word in all its significance, in the totality of its form, tone, warmth, and power. That is what the parable of the seed implies. The sacred Word must be heard, not read. It should reach us through the ears, not through the eyes, as color and form should be seized by the eyes, and not transposed through description. The *how* cannot be separated from the *what*. The word that is written and read silently is different from the fresh, full word of sound. In the process of silent reading, words shrink, their resonant fullness being but poorly substituted by print. If the divine service was meant to be a reading session, books would be distributed; and everyone, priest and faithful, would quietly lose himself in them. The result would be a community of readers. Often we have very little more at Mass, but this is not as it should be. The Word is meant to rise from the sacred page to the reader's lips, from there to swing out into the room, to be heard by attentive ears and received by eager hearts.

Admittedly, there is one great obstacle: the fact that the liturgy is celebrated in a foreign tongue—Latin. We try to overcome this by repeating Epistle and Gospel in English prior to the sermon. But this is a makeshift and usually done only on Sunday. On weekdays as well as on Sundays the faithful are almost entirely dependent on their books. The divine Word ought to reach the hearers simultaneously with its entry into the ceremony of the Mass, but as the liturgy is arranged today, this is impossible.

We must make the best of what we have. Above all, when the English texts are read, we must listen with minds alert and hearts and souls receptive. Such listening is all the more necessary because we've heard the words countless times. We are so used to them that they do not easily impress us. We are convinced that we know all about the Sermon on the Mount, Jesus' parables, or the Epistles, and when they are read we nod as if to say: "All right, all right—I *know*." We must overcome this tendency, or our souls will become like a dirt road over which countless feet and wheels have passed, hard-packed and incapable of receiving a single seed.

The daily changing texts of the Proper—Introit, Offertory, and Communion—often say very little because of their brevity. They have been taken from longer passages (mainly from the Psalms, but also from other parts of Scripture), and it is very helpful to look them up and read them in their entirety. We should read also the Epistle and Gospel more completely in the Bible so as to grasp the context and consult the notes on difficult passages. When they are read aloud in church, we should take great pains to listen attentively; the word of mouth is always more powerful than the word of ink.

14. The Executory Word

The Word of God permeates the whole Mass, as it also fills the entire liturgy. Some of its parts, like the Epistle and Gospel or the Our Father, spoken at the most solemn moments, are larger unbroken passages taken bodily from Scripture. Introit, Offertory, and Collects consist of sentences selected from various biblical books to highlight the significance of the day in question. The same is true of the Gradual and Tract texts which link the Epistle and the Gospel. Finally, in the actual prayers, words from or references to the preceding scriptural quotations return again and again to fortify the whole with their sacred power.

At the heart of the Mass, the Consecration, the Word of the Lord assumes a special character.

Following the Offertory, in which bread and wine are prepared for the sacred feast, is the most important prayer of all: the Canon of the Mass. After the *Quam oblationem*, the Church's final prayer over the gift-offerings, we have the words: "Who the day before he suffered took bread into his holy and venerable hands, and with his eyes lifted up to heaven, unto Thee, God, his almighty Father, giving thanks to Thee, he blessed, broke and gave it to his disciples, saying: Take and eat ye all of this, *for this is My Body*. In like manner, after he had supped, taking also this excellent chalice into his holy and venerable hands, and giving thanks to Thee, he blessed and gave it to his disciples, saying: Take and drink ye all of this, *for this is the Chalice of My Blood, of the new and eternal testament: the mystery of faith: which shall be shed for you and for many unto the remission of sins.* As often as you shall do these things, ye shall do them in remembrance of me."

The words are taken from the Gospel reports and from the First Epistle to the Corinthians. Like the original Epistle and Gospel texts, they seem to repeat, only more impressively, what took place at that time. But when we look closely, we notice slight shifts in the wording. Not only does the priest, by reading the biblical account, relate what took place, he also does it himself. His words are no longer merely the biblical "and giving thanks"; they have become: "and with his eyes lifted up to heaven, unto Thee, God, his almighty Father, giving thanks to Thee . . ." God is actually being addressed. And while the priest says "took bread," he actually picks up the host lying there, bowing his head at the word "thanks." Thus the decisive words, "*for this is my body*" and "*for this is the Chalice of My Blood, of the new and eternal testament: the mystery of faith: which shall be shed for you and for many unto the remission of sins,*" acquire a new character. The whole passage moves from the past into the present, from the report to the act. It is no longer a pious memorial; it has become a living reality. At the consecration of the chalice we were being prepared for something extraordinary: *mysterium fidei*. In the early Church, while the priest softly spoke the words which established the Eucharist, the deacon raised his voice, and reverently called out: "Take heed! The mystery of faith!" It is in this sense that we must receive the Lord's words. But the full significance of their springing into life is clearest in the final sentence: "As often as ye shall do these things, ye shall do them in remembrance of Me."

Here again something happens to the scriptural word which does not happen to the Epistle or Gospel, to the *Pater Noster* or the praises of the *Gloria*. There God's biblical Words are read, proclaimed, and heard; priest and people make them their own and pass them back as prayer to God. Here the Word becomes the living present. What was once spoken by Christ is spoken anew, not as a new Word issuing from the hour and consequently passing away with it, but as the old, Christ-spoken Word renewed and become part of this hour. The "memorial" does not consist in the congregation's remembering what the Lord once spoke to his apostles, but in making his words alive and concretely effective.

We are about to anticipate, but the point to be discussed in detail later is so all-important that it can bear repetition. What Jesus accomplished by these words differed from all the other proofs of his divine omnipotence. Not only was he summoning the powers of creation to the service of the kingdom of God, here, as in the Incarnation and the Resurrection, he was laying the foundations of a new creation. These words are the equals of those which once brought the universe into existence. But it was the Lord's pleasure to permit them their creative task not only once, the evening he spoke them, but from henceforth forever—or as St. Paul says, "until he comes" (1 Cor 11:26). They are meant to ring out ever and again in the course of history, accomplishing each time what they first effected. To this end Christ gave them to his followers with the command: "As often as ye shall do these things, ye shall do them in remembrance of me."

Therefore when the priest utters the words, they are not merely reported but rise and create. Obviously, at this point, we do not simply hear a man talking. The priest pronounces the words, certainly; but they are not his. He is only their bearer; and he does not bear them by reason of his personal faith, piety, or moral strength, but by means of his office, through which he executes the Lord's directions. The true speaker remains Christ. He alone can speak thus. The priest merely lends the Lord his voice, mind, will, and freedom, playing a role similar to that of the baptismal water; for the new birth is not brought about by its natural cleansing qualities, but by the power of Christ. It is Christ who baptizes, just as here it is Christ who speaks.

Our own attitudes should be in keeping with this. It is not merely a question of pious listening and acceptance, nor is it one of consummation in the literal sense of the word. The first would be too little, the second definitely too much. The deacon's interjection in the midst of the holy sentences gives us the right cue: *Mysterium fidei!* The call proclaims the unfolding of the inmost earnestness, the supreme love of God, summoning us to muster all the readiness and power of our faith in order to participate in them.

15. The Word of Praise

We discussed first the revelatory word found chiefly in Epistle and Gospel, as well as in the sermon, and then the executory word which fulfills the Lord's command in the Consecration. There remains the word of prayer. For the most part its nature is obvious, yet there are a few important points that should be made.

Prayer appears in Holy Mass primarily in the impressive form of praise or hymn. Such is the greater doxology or chant of honor, often called the *Gloria,* after its opening word. It begins with the praise of the angels over Bethlehem (see Lk 2:14), continues with expressions lauding God's glory, then shifts to a kind of litany in which the all-holy Persons of the divine Trinity, above all Christ, are supplicated, and ends with the solemn naming of the threefold God.

The part of the Mass known as the Preface is also praise. This introduces the most important prayer of the Mass: the Canon, which includes the Consecration. Indicative of the solemnity of the Preface are its introductory sentences with which priest and people alternately stimulate and strengthen each other's spiritual exaltation. The hymn proper then begins with homage to the Father in heaven, homage based each time on the particular mystery of the feast that is being celebrated. After joining in the glorious praises of the angel-choirs, it terminates with the adoration of the *Sanctus.* The first part of this prayer is taken from the vision of the prophet,

Isaiah, who heard it from the lips of the cherubim (see Is 6:3); the second is from the Gospel passage describing Jesus' entry into Jerusalem, where the exulting children shouted the words to him in the streets (see Mt 21:9).

On certain feast days we find further praises, called Sequences, tucked between Epistle and Gospel. They are hymnal proclamations of the feast's central event, through which they appeal to God. Sequences are to be found mainly in the Masses of Easter, Pentecost, and Corpus Christi.

Sometimes praise, common also in the Graduals, breaks into certain forms of the Introit, Offertory, and Collects (prayers briefly interspersed with alleluias), which are entwined about Epistle and Gospel.

These praises continue the themes of the Psalms and songs of praise in the Old and New Testaments: inspired man, brimming with the experience of God's grandeur, glory and awfulness, with his love and his fervor, proclaims God's omnipotence, admiring, lauding, and worshipping him. The praisegiver lives in this glory as in a special atmosphere in which he delights. The motives for praise vary, but all praise has one thing in common: spiritual exaltation, the glow of divine glory. In praise man's prayer is farthest removed from the everyday world. This sense of the heights is particularly apparent in the prelude to the Preface, in which priest and congregation help each other to leave everything low and mean behind them and to ascend. First they wish each other God's strength: "The Lord be with you," prays the priest, to which the people reply: "And with thy spirit." God is asked to move and fortify his people, to accompany the spirit of his priest. And "spirit" here is not intellect but that simultaneous intimacy and exaltation from which the movements of love, adoration, and enthusiasm climb. Then the priest calls: "Lift up your hearts." The congregation responds: "We have lifted them up unto the Lord." To this comes the new summons: "Let us give thanks to the Lord our God." Response: "It is meet and just." Linked to the last word is the Preface itself: "It is truly meet and just, right and availing unto salvation, that we should at all times and in all places give thanks unto Thee, O holy Lord, Father almighty and everlasting God."

In these lines something peculiar to the prayer of praise is particularly apparent: thanksgiving. It is a rendering of thanks not for some beautiful or useful gift but for the whole of blessed existence. It is man's response to the glory of God unveiled by revelation, man's response to his "Epiphany."

Man thanks his Creator for everything, for everything is his gift: natural life, the gift of creation; supernatural life, that of salvation. Such thanksgiving is the attitude farthest removed from narrowness and selfishness; it is the wide flowering of the heart, the love which embraces the whole breadth of existence, the superabundance of truth. In the *Gloria* it finds its most beautiful expression: "*Gratias agimus tibi propter magnam gloriam tuam.*" "*Gratias agere*" means to thank, honor, and "wish well." Greeks and Romans particularly praised the virtue of magnanimity, the free nobility of being. This attitude appears here in relation to God: "We give thee thanks for Thy great glory." Even in human relationships the feeling exists: "I thank you, not for what you have done for me or for what you think of me, but for yourself, for existing." Here love reaches a mysterious greatness. Actually, thanks for the existence of a loved one should be directed elsewhere: to his parents or to God. What seems folly—albeit beautiful folly—is, when applied to God, pure sense, for he exists of himself. He is the "I am" (Ex 3:14). Of all existences, his alone has "merit," for it is the perfect expression of his love. For this love, man, shaken by God's glory, thanks him.

Deep emotion streams through the songs of praise, emotion different from that of personal experience. Its bearer is not the individual, but the whole, the Church. The Church is more than the sum of her believers, more than the huge *ordo* which enfolds them all. Saints Paul and John tell us what she is: a mighty organism, humanity reborn in the Mystical Body of Christ, in which the individual believers are the pulsing "cells." It is then the Church who speaks in her great hymns.

One might even venture to say that the joy they voice is not hers alone but is shared by God himself. Doesn't St. Paul say that the Holy Spirit himself pleads for us "with unutterable groanings" (Rom 8:26)? If this is true of all prayer, then certainly of the prayer of praise. The Psalms of the Old Testament stream from prophetic enthusiasm; those of the New from the fire of Pentecost. The Acts of the Apostles and the First Epistle to the Corinthians testify to the power of that streaming and storming of the Spirit—so powerful that it shattered the order of thought and speech, so that only a stammering and exclaiming could be recognized. The same Paul, however, admonishes men to restrain such outbursts. Higher than storm and stammer sings the clear word controlled by truth and inner discipline, and the faithful should channel their enthusiasm into "spiritual songs" (1 Cor 12; Eph 5:19). From these spring the hymns of the church. The joy and elation of the spirit which the Father sends us in Christ's name break through and return to the Father. This sense of sacred mounting beats like wings through the hymn sung at the consecration of the paschal candle on Easter Saturday, the "Exultet," but it is also perceptible in the *Gloria* and in other songs of praise.

The word of revelation demands of us composed listening and pious absorption; the executory word of the Consecration, our reverent presence and participation. The word of praise asks to become our own, that we give it our best or rather ourselves that we let it sweep us along with it, teaching us what real prayer is that we may outgrow the narrowness and pettiness of self.

We can only repeat: It would be a good preparation for Holy Mass to go over the *Gloria* or a Gradual or Preface the day before, or before the service begins, to enable these to come alive for us and to allow us to recognize and practice the exaltation that each contains.

16. THE WORD OF ENTREATY

In singular contrast to the prayer of praise stands the prayer of entreaty, the *oratio*. We find it chiefly in three places: after the *Gloria* in the Collects, after the Offertory in the Secret, and after the Communion prayer in the Postcommunion. It also appears in the Canon (in the various requests before and after the Consecration) and at the end of the Our Father. Our concern here is with the prayers which appear in the three places mentioned first: the Collect, the Secret, and the Postcommunion.

That they are important is at once seen from the words and gestures which precede them. The priest kisses the altar, an expression of closest contact with the place of God's proximity; then he turns to the people and with a grave and formal gesture says: "The Lord be with you." To this the congregation or server replies: "And with thy spirit." It is the same words of collectedness and strengthening we met before in the Preface. The Priest says: "*Oremus*—let us pray." And the Collect follows. The preamble of the Secret is even more solemn. There the priest says first: "*Orate, fratres*—Brethren, pray," then he continues: "that my sacrifice and yours may be acceptable to God the Father almighty." The server answers: "May the Lord receive the Sacrifice at thy hands, to the praise and glory of his name, to our own benefit, and to that of all his holy Church." After this preparation the priest prays over the offerings lying on the altar.

In all these prayers we are struck by one thing: their strict formality. They are terse and austere, the more so the older they are. Here are no elaborate thoughts, no moving images, no emotional outpourings. Nothing but a few clear, terse sentences.

An example is found in the Collect for the first Monday in Lent: "Convert us, O God our salvation, and that the Lenten fast may be of profit to us, instruct our minds with heavenly discipline." And the Secret from the same Mass: "Sanctify, O Lord, the gifts offered to Thee: and cleanse us from the stains of our sins." Finally the Postcommunion: "Filled with the gift of Thy salvation, we humbly beseech Thee, O Lord, that even as we rejoice in the participation thereof, we may be renewed also by its effect."

At first the tone seems foreign to us. Our prayers are usually wordier. There is more emotion in them, and they are far more personal. Of course, not all the prayers of the Mass are as austere as these, which have come down to us from a very early period, but their general tenor is more or less the same. The more subjective prayer is always of a later origin and somehow has lost its reserve. The early prayers spring not from the personal experience of the individual, but from the consciousness of the congregation, or, more exactly, of the Church. Often they are very official, in the original sense of the word: the outcome of the *officium*, duty, the charges of office. Roman clarity and objectivity so dominate them that to us of another stamp and era they often seem cool and impersonal—perhaps even unreligious. But in this we should be very much mistaken, for they are packed with a piety both powerful and profound; it is only that their form is different from that to which we are accustomed. They are not really alien to us, as Chinese rites would be; no matter how earnestly we took the latter, they would never touch us personally, never become one with our spirit. The early Christian prayers belong to us; they are a profound part of us. They come from the opposite pole of our existence, and we need them if we are to exist as complete persons. Inclined as we are to lose ourselves in the irrelevant and the all-too-subjective, their clear-cut objective piety maintains an important balance.

We cannot grasp the significance of these texts without real effort. They are the fruit of deep concentration. An alert sense of reality has experienced life; an unclouded mind has recognized and seized upon the essential; precise and telling expression has made possible their complete simplicity. The history of the first centuries best reveals the masterly grasp of reality that forms the basis of these prayers; for the young Church had to struggle heroically, first with the voluptuous luxury of a decaying antiquity, then with the mighty forces that came into existence in the chaos of the great migrations and of the dawning Middle Ages. They are not, as we might suppose, complete self-explanatory texts; the situation from which they spring was summed up in the silent prayers that preceded them. We do not take the introductory "Let us pray" seriously enough. The procedure really should be as follows: Folding his hands, the priest says: "*Oremus*—let us pray." Now there is silence for a good while, during which the individual believer, taking the mystery of the day as his theme, prays for his own intention and for the intention of the congregation. This silent, manifold praying is then gathered up by the priest and expressed in the few sentences of the Collect, so that its brief words are filled with all the vitality that has just silently lifted itself to God. Now its terseness no longer seems inadequate, but rich and recapitulative. By studying the Collects beforehand, we could make them the vehicles of our intentions, as they were meant to be.

These prayers are significant for the direction that prayer takes in them. The catechism defines prayer as a lifting of the heart to God, for God is above us and our way to him leads upward. He is also in us; so the way to him leads through the inner sanctuary. How does this movement take place? Has it some guiding principle or method? All Collects, regardless of content, close with a remarkable sentence: "Through our Lord Jesus Christ, Who livest and reignest with God the Father in the unity of the Holy

Ghost, God, world without end." Here is the direction we were seeking, the proper relation between the goal, the way, and the power that enables us to take it. The goal is the Father; prayer is a seeking of his face. The way is Christ. The power is the Holy Spirit. This one sentence contains the whole law of liturgical prayer. Its method is the same used by the divine Trinity in the work of our salvation. All things come from and return to the Father. In the *Logos*, he created the world. When man sinned, Christ was sent into the world to rescue and restore it to the Father. The power by which the eternal Son became man and fulfilled his task was that of the Holy Spirit. In the strength of this same Spirit, sent us by the Father in the Son's name, we return along the road of Christ home to the Father. We are Christians in Christ. Our new life is life-in-Him. Hence Christian prayer is prayer in Christ.

By this time the attentive reader will have noticed that almost invariably the liturgy unrolls before the Father, to whom all words and acts are addressed. Very rarely, and then only for an obvious reason, does it turn to the Son: for instance in the *Gloria*, where one of the holy Persons after the other is invoked, or in the *Agnus Dei*, as the priest's eyes seem to meet those of the Savior offering himself for sacrifice. The prayers of later periods are more inclined to address themselves to Christ, but we feel at once that somehow they are out of order. The holy Countenance to which the words of the liturgy are directed is that of the Father; but at every point Christ is the vital "room" in which everything takes place and the way that is taken. His revelation is the Truth that meets us wherever we look. His living, dying, and rising again is the power that lifts all things into newness. His living reality is the model for, and the manner of, holy existence, the essential to which we should surrender ourselves and in which we should exist. The Holy Spirit is the power by which we are meant to accomplish both the oneness with Christ and the movement toward the Father.

All this is of vital importance. It is the very principle of Christian existence. It is so true and so fundamental that it does not particularly force itself upon the consciousness. We hardly notice it until we turn to the later prayers that someone has, at some time or another, felt called upon to compose, and we suddenly notice how cramped we feel in them. The most important things pass unnoticed. They belong to the *a priori* of existence and are lived in rather than regarded: air, light, the arrangement of space and time, the ground on which we stand, and the way from our particular point of departure to the goal. We do not notice how essential they are until they are missing. The principle we have been discussing is somewhat analogous, only incomparably greater and holier. It is the working principle of truth and love by which God himself lives, creates, and redeems. It is to this that he summons us; our praying is meant to be fulfilled according to its sacred law.

17. The Congregation and Injustice Rectified

The word *congregation* does not mean a gathering of many people—not even of many pious and reverent people. Even in such a group, that unifying, simultaneously fortifying, and fervent quality, which is the essence of the true congregation, might be lacking. Christ defines it: "For where two or three are gathered together for my sake, there am I in the midst of them" (Mt 18:20). The Acts of the Apostles gives more details in its report on the days following Pentecost: "And continuing daily with one accord in the temple, and breaking bread in their houses, they took their food with gladness and simplicity of heart, praising God and being in favor with all the people" (Acts 2:46–47). A congregation exists when a number of people disciplined by faith and conscious of their membership in Christ gather to celebrate the sacred mysteries. Even then it does not follow effortlessly. There are a few exceptions when it does seem to—for instance, when an oppressive need or powerful joy spontaneously fills and fuses all hearts; or when the words of an inspired teacher have moved the hearers to genuine Christian *unitas*, making of the many individuals one great body drawn by the same power to the same end. But as a rule congregation exists only when its members will it. Many things can help: the solemnity of the room, organ music, the power of the divine word, and the earnestness and mystery of the sacred ceremony. But these can only help, they cannot do everything; from the standpoint of our personal responsibility, they are unable to achieve even the main thing. For a congregation must be possible also without these: in uninspiring surroundings; with the feeblest music or none at all; with the sacred word inadequately proclaimed; a divine service to which all possible human shortcomings cling. Above all, if there is to be a congregation, the believers must know what a congregation is; they must desire it and actively strive to attain it.

In the Sermon on the Mount the Lord says: "Therefore, if thou art offering thy gift at the altar, and there rememberest that thy brother has anything against thee, leave thy gift before the altar and go first to be reconciled to thy brother, and then come and offer thy gift" (Mt 5:23–24). This means when you go to Mass and you recall that you have been unjust to someone and that he bears you a grudge, you cannot simply walk into church as though nothing were wrong. For then you would be entering only the physical room of the building, not the congregation, which would not receive you, as you would destroy it by your mere presence. A congregation is the sacred coherence which links person to person as it links God to men and men to God. It is the unity of men *in Christ*—in the living Christ "in the midst of them," before the countenance of his Father, in the efficacy of the Holy Spirit. But if you have wronged your "brother," and he has a grudge against you, a wall rises between you and him that excludes you from the sacred unity; then, as far as you are concerned, congregation ceases to exist. It is your responsibility to restore it by removing the impediment between you and your brother.

You cannot very well go about it as the Sermon on the Mount in its divine simplicity advises: simply by dropping everything, going to the one you have wronged and rectifying things, then returning. Perhaps we shouldn't be so hasty with our "cannots." We can do much more than we suppose, and our bourgeois, watered-down Christian existence would be strengthened if we would more often act with the directness of the believing heart, would simply go and do what love and repentance and magnanimity dictate. I am not lauding impulsiveness; I am only trying to suggest that reflection is sometimes a hindrance, and that often the necessary, truly liberating act is possible only through the power and momentum of the first impulse.

Be this as it may, anyone who knows that somewhere someone has something against him certainly can do one thing: he can promise himself to remove the injustice by correcting it as soon as possible. The honest intention suffices to bring down the wall between himself and his brother. Immediately the unifying element is free again to contact all parts. As soon as the injustice that isolates has been overcome, the congregation is restored.

Jesus' word can also be reversed. We can say: "Therefore, if thou art offering thy gift at the altar, and there rememberest that thou hast any-thing against thy brother, leave thy gifts before the altar and go first to be reconciled to thy brother, and then come and offer thy gift." Here you are the one with the complaint. Now you can act much more directly. For the essential depends not on the actual agreement reached by the estranged parties but on one condition: your forgiveness. As long as you bear your grudge, no matter how "valid," there can be no true congregation as far as you are concerned. Forgive, honestly and sincerely, and the sacred unifying circle will close again. Perhaps this is impossible all at once. Sometimes disappointment and revolt are too great to permit genuine forgiveness right away. Then forgive as much as is in your power and ask God to give you an increase of forgiveness. For it is not man who effects true forgiveness. The commandment to forgive one's enemies might have been expressed: "Know that thou canst forgive thy enemy because Christ on the cross forgave His; it is he who effects forgiveness in thee." Human forgiveness is different from that which the Lord meant. It could be mere prudence, which says: "Let it go—nothing will come of it anyway"; or indifference: "What does it matter?"; or false friendliness, which is no more than inverted dislike;

or cowardice, which does not trust itself to fight it out, and so forth. The forgiveness of Christ is different. It means that divine love gains a footing in us, creating that new order which is meant to reign among the sons and daughters of God. Hence when you try to fulfill the law of love for the sake of God and his holy mysteries, you make it possible for God to allow the congregation of those rooted in his love to flower.

18. The Congregation
and the Church

When churchgoers enter the sacred precincts, they come as individuals, each with his particular talents and circumstances, worries and wishes. Each takes his own stand, confronting the others. Each is isolated from the others by all the sentiments summed up in the words "I—not you": indifference, strangeness, mistrust, superiority, dislike, and enmity; by the hard crust developed in the struggle for existence and by the disappointments that past goodwill has experienced. This is the mental state of the average worshipper as he steps into church, stands or sits or kneels; certainly there is as yet little of the "member of a congregation" about him. Leaving aside the questionable and the out-and-out wrong that this state brings with it—lovelessness, pride, ill will, and so forth—let us try to get an idea of the kind of life that is pouring into the church. We have a roomful of people, each with his private thoughts, feelings, and aims—a conglomeration of little separate worlds. The bearing of everyone present seems to say "I" or at best the "we" of his closest associations: his family, friends, or dependents. But even this inclusion often really means little more than a widened self-esteem. The singular ego is stretched to a natural group ego that is still far removed from genuine congregation. The true congregation is a gathering of those who belong to Christ, the holy people of God, united by faith and love. Essentially, it is of his making, a piece of new creation, which finds expression in the bearing of its participants.

When we read the prayers of the Mass with this in mind, we notice that the word "I" appears very seldom and never without a special reason. It is found quite clearly in the prayers at the foot of the altar when each one present acknowledges his sins; in the *Credo*, when the individual, conscious of his personal responsibility, professes his belief in divine revelation; in the prayers immediately preceding Holy Communion.[9] As a rule, "we" is used. We praise thee, we glorify thee, we adore thee; forgive us, help us, enlighten us. This "we" is not spontaneous but the carefully nurtured fruit of genuine congregation.

Now we begin to see what we are after: not a communal "experience"; not the individual's great, joyous, or overwhelming foretaste of the union of many before God, which may sometime sweep through him, filling and sustaining him. Like all true experience that is a gift of the hour, which is given or withheld, it cannot be merited. Here though it is a question not of an experience but of an accomplishment, not of a gift but of a required deed.

If we are to get anywhere with these considerations, we must realize how deeply immersed in self we are and—for all our talk of community— what thorough egoists. When we speak of community we seldom mean more than the experience of self-extension. Lifted up and out of our personal narrowness by the total vitality around us, we feel suddenly stronger or more enthusiastic than otherwise. In reality, no matter how long and how often people are together, they always remain alone. The real antonym of community is not the individual and his individualism but the egoist and his selfishness. It is this that must first be overcome, and not by frequent or prolonged association but by mastering the mind and will, which alone allows us to see others as they really are: to acknowledge and accept them, to make their desires and anxieties our own, and to restrain ourselves for their sakes. But to do this we must have solitude, for only in solitude do we have a chance to see ourselves objectively and to free ourselves from our own chains. Someday, perhaps on some special occasion, we will realize what walls of indifference, disregard, and enmity loom between us and "the other man," and before Mass or during the Introit we will make a real effort to break through them. We will remind ourselves: "Together we face God; together we are congregation. Not only I and others in general, but this man, that woman over there, and the believer next to me. In God's sight they are all as important as I—perhaps much more so: purer, braver, less selfish, nobler, more loving and fervent. Among these people whom I know only by their features and by their gestures, are perhaps great and holy souls with whom I am fortunate to find myself associated, because the surge of their prayers sweeps me along with it to God!"

Then we will let the other believers into the inner circles of our lives; present ourselves to God with them, linking our intentions to theirs. We will consciously, earnestly pray the "we" of the liturgy, for from such things congregation is formed.

Until now we have spoken of congregation as the Christian "we" in its encounter with God, the community of those united by the same faith and by mutual love. But this is not all. The conception must include also those outside any particular building, even outside the Church; for congregation reaches far beyond. It is no closed circle, no organization or union with its own center; each congregation is part of a whole that far surpasses any Sunday gathering. It embraces everyone who believes in Christ in the same city, the same country, over the whole earth. The congregation gathered in any one church is influenced by its particular circumstances, by its services, by the quality of its members, and by the particular feats that they are celebrating. It is a unit, but one that remains open; and all who are bound to Christ are included in it. Its center is the altar, every altar in every church—altar that is simultaneously the center of the world. At Christ's table all the faithful are remembered, and all belong to the "we" that is spoken there.

And still we have not touched bottom. In the *Confiteor* priest and faithful confess their sins. Their confession is addressed primarily to God, and in his presence alternately to each other, but it is also addressed to Mary, the Mother of the Lord, to the archangel Michael, to John the Baptist, to the apostles Peter and Paul, and to all the saints. Behind the archangel, who appears here as the leader of the heavenly hosts, stands the world of the angels; and "the saints" means not only the great historical figures of sanctity that the word usually suggests, but all the saved, all who have "gone home" to God. In other parts of the Mass as well, those who already participate in eternal life are invoked, whereas in the memento for the dead after the consecration all those still in need of purification and prayer are remembered.

In other words, congregation stretches not only over the whole earth but also far beyond the borders of death. About those gathered around the altar the horizons of time and space roll back, revealing as the real, sustaining community the whole of saved humanity.

This congregation *in toto* then is the Church, sustainer of the holy act of worship. That the Mass is something quite different from the private religious act of an individual is obvious, but it is also more than the divine service of a group of individuals united by like beliefs, that of a sect, for instance. It is the Church with all the breadth that the word implies—the universal Church. We begin to visualize her scope when we read what Saints Paul and John write of her. There, even her ultimate earthly limits dissolve to make her one with all saved creation. Her attributes are "the new man," "the new heaven," and "the new earth!"

Nor is the Church merely the sum total of the saved plus the totality of things, but a living unit, an "organism" formed and composed round a reigning, all-permeating figure: the spiritual Christ. She has full powers to proclaim Christ's teaching and bestow his sacraments; respect or disrespect to her involves God himself. What sustains the Mass are not only an endless legion of hearts and spirits, the faith and love of all creation, but also a supernatural society endowed with authority and bearing responsibilities.

Our task is to find our place in the enormous whole. This is not easy. Man has a leaning to spiritual intimacy and exclusiveness, which causes him to shrink from such magnitude and grandeur. There is also the resistance of modern religious feeling to the visible Church in its realistic sense: resistance to office and order, to authority and constitutionality. We are all-too-subjective, inclined to count as truly religious only the direct and spontaneous experience. Order and authority leave us cold. Here self-discipline is especially necessary. The text of the Mass repeatedly reveals the attitude which has been called "Roman," an attitude that rests precisely upon the consciousness of formal institutional unity, God-given authority, law, and order. This may strike us as strange, perhaps even as unreligious—we spoke of this before in our discussion of the Collects. Those same Collects express something very important for us. Not only are we as Christians "congregation," not only "saved mankind" and "new creation"; we ourselves *are* "Church," so we must consent and patiently educate ourselves to this given role.

19. Hindrance: Habit

This book is called *Meditations before Mass* and its aim is to present for reflection—each time from a different angle—thoughts inducive to a fuller participation in the sacred celebration. Part One now draws to a close with a few purely practical considerations. What actually hinders us from taking part in the Mass as we should? First of all, habit.

It is fundamental spiritual law that every impression exhausts itself. All life is a perpetual becoming but also a perpetual perishing; thus an impression starts out strong, gains in strength, lasts for a while, then fades. He who has experienced it has "used it up," and indifference sets in. This is as it should be as long as it is a question of the many fleeting contacts of daily life; each has its moment or moments and then makes way for the next. But the same process becomes fatal when permitted to govern relations that are a fundamental part of our existence and consequently irreplaceable: our vocation, for instance, with its unchanging demands and responsibilities; marriage; genuine friendship; or our relations to self, since we are as we are and must find some sort of *modus vivendi* with ourselves. Here the law of diminishing impressions and emotions can cause serious difficulties. When a task is new and full of interest, it seems to perform itself. When it has been performed for a long time, it becomes burdensome and difficult. The company of another person is joyful and stimulating as long as yet unknown responses in his thinking or surprises in his attitude refresh us;

but after closer acquaintance, when we begin to know beforehand exactly how we will react and reply, boredom sets in. As for ourselves, we all have experienced discouragement with our shortcomings and oppressive disgust with our own nature.

All this applies to Holy Mass as well. We hear it every Sunday; many people more often, even daily. It is always pretty much the same, most of the principal texts recurring time and again. Always it begins with the same prayers at the altar steps, varied on certain occasions only by the omission of the psalm *Judica me*. In accordance with the Lord's command to do in his memory what he himself did, the Canon too, with slight variations, remains the same: the great prayer-texts, *Kyrie*, *Gloria*, *Credo*, *Pater Noster* and *Agnus Dei* are complete units that never change. Sometimes the *Gloria* is omitted (during Advent and Lent) or the *Credo* is left out, as in certain weekday Masses, or in those commemorating the martyrs, confessors, and holy women. Even the variable parts of the Mass resemble one another in construction, language, and spiritual attitude. The Graduals, for example, are usually patterned after the biblical proverbs and interspersed with alle-lujas. The Collect always begins with the direct address, then develops the principal thought, and finishes off with the formal end-clause. In time, even the changing Epistle and Gospel readings lose their freshness. After years of following the sacred ceremony, we begin to respond to it as to an old, familiar friend.

Thus at first fleetingly, then ever more prolonged and powerfully, the feeling of monotony creeps in. "I know all that. I know exactly what words follow every move." When in addition the same priest appears at the same altar over a long period, officiating in the same manner with his unchang-ing personal peculiarities and shortcomings, a veritable crisis of boredom and weariness can overcome us. We no longer "get anything out of it," hardly know why we still go. The fact that Church law requires Sunday attendance sometimes only adds to our difficulties.

What shall we do? Stay away? When the Mass threatens to become a habit for someone who goes regularly during the week, it is certainly advisable for him to attend less frequently, perhaps only on Sundays for a while, substituting visits in the quiet church or Bible reading. But this remedy is not possible for the Sunday churchgoer, whose attendance is required on that day. Here is an illustration of the pedagogic importance of this precept: our nature requires a rule that will keep us from giving up entirely.

It is claimed that religious life must come from within and should not be forced, yet man lives not only spontaneously but also in the practice and discipline of an ordered existence. Whenever he abandons these, something valuable is lost. The rule about Sunday attendance is therefore not only necessary but right, the more so as it applies to sacred time, the day of the Lord and its relation to the rest of the week. But behind the pedagogical standpoint is another and more important consideration: the fact that Christ instituted the mystery of the Mass, so that it is not something we can ignore at whim but the essential core of our religious life. And if we really were to omit it, what should we put in its place? We would devise something of our own choosing and soon experience a much worse satiety: the insupportable triviality of human endeavor where the ultimate meaning of existence is at stake.

Then what can we do? First, make it clear to ourselves once and for all that Holy Mass belongs in our lives. In the conviction of a thing's finality and inalterability lies a peculiar strength. As soon as I am convinced that I should perform some act, I can do it—at least up to a certain point. Anything but steadfast by nature, man is always ready to let things slide; this definite law in his life is something like the bones in his body, giving him firmness and character.

"Sing ye to the Lord a new canticle." The psalm does not mean that the singer must continually hope for new inspiration, but that all his singing should soar fresh from the heart renewed. This power of renewal is one of the happiest elements of life, the ability not only to create something nonexistent but also to recreate something that already exists in so new a way that it seems to exist for the first time. Man *is* capable of breaking through the monotony of long continued doing and seeing, and, by inner readiness, of beginning anew.

This is particularly true of Holy Mass, which is something absolute and inexhaustible. Much of it is the work of men—in the beautiful sense of the word, as God-directed human service, as well as in the pejorative sense of formalism and superficiality. Its central reality, however, is the saving act of the living Christ, which contains the fullness of God's wisdom and love, not merely as objects received, but as vital and operative forces. At the celebration of the Lord's memorial we are not dependent on our own faculties of perceiving and appreciating; Christ works with us. Primarily it is he who acts; in our "remembering" it is Christ himself who stirs.

Habituality and monotony best prove that things, activities, and people have only a certain measure of significance and reality; hence at some time or other that measure will be full and there will be nothing new to add; then stimulating interest must be replaced by loyalty. In the Mass, however, it is different. Here we are dealing directly with Christ and his work of salvation, with the *Logos*, and with the infinitude of his divine being and the inexhaustibility of his love. We are here related to Christ not only in the sense that he demands from us his just due; he helps us with the work of commemoration. Faith tells us that monotony cannot come from what the Mass itself is; it can make its appearance, but only in us, when we do not take Christ and his love seriously enough. Christ is new precisely to the extent that the believer occupies himself with him. Every act of obedience, every self-conquest, and every situation in life that we master through the Lord's direction and strength reveals something new in him. The Mass gives as much as we ask of it. And the power of renewal is not limited to our own capacity for renewal; we can count upon God's infinite possibilities.

Admittedly, we can claim this only in faith, but the truth of what is believed becomes apparent to the extent that it is personally experienced.

20. Hindrance: Sentimentality

To put it bluntly, sentimentality is essentially the desire to be moved: by loneliness or delight, sorrow or dread; by greatness and exaltedness or weakness and helplessness—somehow to be moved. The need is greater with one person than with another, but we all have it to some extent. Strangely enough, it is particularly dominant in people who do not appear at all emotional: self-disciplined men of intellect and will and practical, prosaic natures. From this we see that sentimentality is not the same as real sentiment, which is powerful, unclouded, and chaste. Sentimentality is a half sentiment, a spiritual softness tinged with sensuality. Hence it is strong not only in people without a clear-cut genuine sense of values but also in those who seem to stand completely on "character," with emphasis leaning so heavily on will and discipline that their neglected feelings easily slide off into the questionable and inferior.

All this has its parallel in the religious life. The sentimental believer's attitude to the great figures of sanctity, the truths he prefers, the passages he frequently quotes, his whole bearing, everything disposes him to emotionalism.

Up to a certain point there is little that can be said against this; it is simply a predisposition, like a fuzzy mind or weak muscles. But when a believer allows such a tendency to dominate him, it becomes disastrous, robbing revelation of its greatness, distorting the saints, and generally rendering his religious life soft, weak, unnatural, and embarrassing. Examples of sentimentality meet us everywhere; we've only to glance at the popular spiritual-exercise leaflets, the average samples of "religious art," or to read some of the meditations on Christ's passion or on the poor souls in purgatory. One theme in particular has fallen under this deplorable influence: the Sacred Heart. By rights this devotion belongs to the profoundest level of Christian piety. Its expression should be huge with the magnitude of revealed truth and vibrant with the power of Christ's conviction. It should be noble and pure. Instead, it is only too often characterized by an intolerable effeminacy and unnaturalness.

Much more could be said on the subject. At any rate, sentimentality is a force that must be reckoned with. For the sentimental believer, participation in the Mass is extremely difficult. He finds the sacred act neither comforting nor edifying but austere, coldly impersonal, and almost forbidding. And for people like himself he is right. The Mass is austere. Its tremendous concepts are expressed tersely. Its action is simple. Its words are clear and concise; its emotion controlled. Its spiritual attitude is that of profoundest surrender, but still and chaste. Sentimentality tries to gild the lily by transferring its own trimmings to the Mass. The altar, never meant to depart far from the pure form of the sacred table, becomes a pompous welter of cherubs and little lamps and much glitter; the action is garlanded with gestures contrived above all to touch the emotions; the servers' apparel is fussy and doll-like. Texts and music are of an ingratiating sweetness. In place of the missal's powerful language, we find Mass "devotions" abounding in artificial conceptions and soft, unnatural sentiments. Thus the central truth of the Mass is lost. The Lord's memorial becomes an "edifying" exhibition, and earnest participation in the sacred ceremony is supplanted by a touching "experience."

The event that took place at the Last Supper in Jerusalem and the death that the Lord died on the cross—both mysteriously interwoven, as his own words reveal—are renewed again and again. Christ commanded:

"As often as ye shall do these things, ye shall do them in remembrance of me" (see 1 Cor 11:25). The Church accepted the command, obeying it through the centuries to the end of time. How does she "do them"? In the strict form of the liturgy.

How would such doing look had it been left to the religious sentiments—if not downright sentimentalities—of the pious? To have an idea, we really should examine some of the devotional leaflets. Everything would be extremely wordy and moving, the fearful and gruesome aspects of suffering would be stressed wherever possible, and Jesus' love would be the constantly reiterated theme. A pious importunity would accost him, praise and pity him, place all sorts of touching phrases in his mouth. The texts of the missal speak quite differently. They are clear and concise. Their tone is that of profound emotion, dignified and controlled. Jesus himself is hardly addressed. Not at all during the Canon; briefly after the completion of the act of commemoration—in the *Agnus Dei* and in the prayers before Communion—and always with great reserve. As a rule, the words of the Mass are addressed to the Father. There is no mention at all of the Lord's feelings during his passion and dying. Veiled in deepest reverence, they stand mute behind the whole mystery.

As for the sacred action, we see from the Passion plays how the sentiments of the believers would have developed it: in the direction of an elaborate mimicry of what took place in the room of the Last Supper and on Golgotha. When we consider the alternatives, we begin to realize what divine powers were necessary to create something as truly God inspired as the Mass is.

Here is neither mimicry nor sentimental, vicarious experience. What took place on Golgotha does not come to the fore at all, but remains eloquently silent behind the whole. The action is taken from the event in the Supper chamber, again not imitated but translated into a strict, stylized form that conceals as much as it reveals. The early Christians believed that it was proper to clothe the sacred in mystery. One reason for their attitude was the danger of persecution, which profaned it at every opportunity; but they also knew that mystery is the natural element of holiness. This element has been lost to us or allowed to sink into the twilight of emotionalism and false mysticism. Possibly one of the most pressing tasks of the religious renewal is to rediscover genuine mystery and the attitude it requires, an attitude that has nothing sentimental about it and that flatly refuses to "facilitate" the demands of faith, preferring to guard its full austerity and dignity. The only genuine arcane discipline still in existence may be found and acquired in the liturgy alone.

The strict form of the Mass aims at the exact opposite of what sentimentality desires. Sentimentality, desirous of being moved, employs to this end stirring gestures evocative of terror and helplessness, words dripping with feeling, exciting imagery, moving dialogue, and the like. Nothing of all this is to be found in the Mass; thus the sentimental believer has three choices: he can relinquish all hope of establishing vital contact with the Mass and retire into his own sphere of private devotions; he can falsify its character, turning it into a kind of moving Passion Play; or he can courageously face his inclinations and bring them to heel. Sentimentality must be overcome; otherwise genuine contact with the Mass is impossible. The individual must discard once and forever the habit of judging it from his personal leanings and tastes, for its form is that which obedience to the Lord's command has received from his Church. Of course, here too exaggeration must be avoided. Neither her ceremonies nor their wording should assume the absoluteness of dogmas; but this much is certain: the manner in which the Lord's memorial is executed in the Church is the *lex orandi*, the norm of divine service. He who really wishes to believe—in other words, to obey revelation—must obey also in this, schooling his private sentiments on that norm. Then it will be clear to him that here a spiritual life of quite different dimensions from that of his personal piety is at work. He will come to know feeling that emerges from the profundity of

God. He will enter the inner realm of Christ. He will experience in himself the powers that govern the inner life of the Church.

21. Hindrance: Human Nature

How exactly, did the Lord institute the mystery of the Eucharist? Considering what was happening, who was placing the essence of his being and work into an act which henceforth, constantly renewed, was to form the center of religious existence, one would suppose that he minutely determined everything—the structure of the whole as well as the details of words and action and that he protected this holy of holies from the disturbing and distorting effects of history by placing it in a spiritual "preserve" guarded by strict laws. The more so since the Old Testament tradition from which he came had developed an elaborate cult life, so that on the one hand he would find such specification only natural, on the other he would consider it necessary in order to keep the line between the old and the new clear and definite. Yet actually it was quite different. The Gospel reports show that Christ was completely filled with the significance of the moment. It is unthinkable that he could have been careless of anything. He does precisely what he set out to do. But what is that? In connection with the Passover feast, he takes bread, pronounces over it the words we know, and offers it to his followers to eat. He does the same with the chalice. He says: "As often as ye shall do these things, ye shall do them in remembrance of me." It is plain whom he means: the apostles and their successors. What they must do is also evident: "these things" that he himself has just done, without warping or "spiritualizing" them. That is all. Nothing more is said: no instructions on how the act is to be worked out in detail, its position in a greater whole or frame, when and where it is to be performed, and all the other questions which naturally arise. Thus the terse command of infinite possibilities and divine dignity is laid with startling simplicity in human hands.

Jesus drew upon the situation of the Passover for the sacred act and commanded that in the future it continue to be celebrated in this new form. In brief, he arranged no proceedings; he planted a seed, which promptly took root in the young congregation and unfolded there. The Church has always known that what took place on Maundy Thursday was to be renewed in the celebration of the Eucharist: not in the form of mimicry but as a vital realization. The seed has always been directly affected by its "soil"—by all the forces, motives, and circumstances that affected its growth, again by the size of the congregation, by its urban or rural location, by the kind of people in it and the historical and cultural situation in which they found themselves.

Thus the cornerstone of the sacred act was laid in history—and what a long and diversified history! There could not fail to appear along with its vital, indestructible aspects, others bound to prove transitory, soon to become extinct. The whole structure had to "settle" sometime in the process, shifting certain concepts out of-line. Sometimes less valuable additions managed to creep into language or ritual, and there were other dangers, quite aside from the hazards of the "dead language" employed.

Another thing: Holy Mass is celebrated by people, by a priest and servers and the congregation. All are human. One is deeply appreciative of the special nature and form of the liturgy; another is not. One responds easily to symbols; another only to ideas or moral precepts. Even within a single individual the degrees of readiness and spiritual participation fluctuate. There are alert and joyous periods, but also periods of indifference and despondency, carelessness and dullness. God's sacred act is planted in human imperfection. Celebrated by a priest for whom the liturgy is really alive, its words and gestures are convincing; they are apt to appear forced and unnatural in one who is not immersed in the spirit of the liturgy. Then there are all the private, little shortcomings of speech and bearing and movement that can be so distracting. The same is true of the congregation. It too can be understanding or indifferent, can actively participate or merely allow events to take their course. It can be educated to the celebration of the Mass and really understand; but it can also passively watch the ceremony unwind, an accepted tradition, day after day, Sunday after Sunday. It can enter into the sacred action or remain outside, carrying on its private devotion with all the varying shades of mood that ever variable human life contains.

For the individual believer this can present serious difficulties. When he goes to Holy Mass he finds it as it is with all its inadequacies. Everything depends on whether he remains a spectator who expects to be "offered something decent"—and is accordingly pleased or disappointed—or whether he understands that it is a question of service performed together, hence depending not only on the priest and the rest of the congregation but also on himself.

Everyone is responsible for the celebration of the Mass, each according to his qualifications. As far as he is able to act within the established order, the individual should do everything in his power to perfect a practice or remove an abuse. Beyond that, he must accept the Mass he attends as it happens to be. He must not be unduly upset by its limitations; certainly he must not use them as an excuse to withhold his share of participation. He should remind himself that the essential remains untouched, should enter into it, and help to accomplish the sacred act.

Part Two

The Essence of the Mass

Prefatory Note to Part Two

This book is intended to help prepare the reader for genuine participation in Holy Mass. Part One was concerned with the attitude necessary to allow for and preserve full participation; Part Two considers the Lord's memorial itself, not for the sake of theoretical information but in order to prepare us for the holy act.

As the subject matter in both parts is so closely related, it is impossible to avoid repetitions. When a thought is needed in some particular context, the reader cannot be expected to look it up in another. Moreover, repetitions are justified in a book whose practical aims have been frequently emphasized, for its intention is to guide the reader to correct doing, which is always a question of practice and consequently of repetition.

—R.G.

22. The Institution

Religious life is the life which ties man to God. It is not mere knowledge or experience of God, but actual union with him. God exists. Man also exists, but his existence is only through God and in his sight. From God to man and from man to God runs a bond more real and more vital than any bond uniting one being with another on earth. This bond between God and man, its effects on man's experience, thought, and action is our religious life.

Religious life can take a double direction. It can enter into our daily living and doing and struggling, into our relations with people and things, and into our work and "works." One man tries to fulfill God's will by accepting and performing his given job with a strict sense of duty; another, reluctant to break a divine commandment, refuses to inflict an injustice; a third practices heroic patience and helpfulness toward someone in the love of Christ. All this is genuine religious life. All three attitudes are proofs of religious sincerity. In them religion has become the soul of daily existence—what Scripture calls "walking in the sight of God."

But religious life can also detach itself from daily existence and seek God directly. The individual believer may turn away from external doings and happenings to meditate on divine revelation; he may take his concerns to God; he may appear "before" God to examine his own acts from God's perspective and renew himself in virtue. Or a whole congregation may assemble in a room that even externally expresses its detachment from ordinary life in order to receive the sacred word, to worship God in common, and to place their intentions at his feet.

Both forms are good; indeed they support each other. In the immediate religious act man collects himself; enlightened and strengthened, he returns to daily existence with a higher degree of readiness. What he experiences there in the way of work, struggle, and destiny causes the new need that sends him gravely back to the sanctuary, to receive fresh light and aid. The demands of daily existence on their part constantly test the genuineness of a man's religion, enabling him to recognize mere pious sentiment and irrelevant fantasy for what they are.

Holy Mass belongs in the second category of religious life. It is not only "one of the ways" of turning directly to God but is the heart of the direct relationship between God and believer. When the Christian goes to church, he leaves the world of ordinary human existence behind and steps into the hallowed spot set apart for God. There he remains with the others of the congregation, a living offerer of the sacred service celebrated before God's countenance.

Once more it is essential for us to make distinctions. What we do in this area reserved for God does not spring directly from our religious experience or desire; neither do we all gather in church to express to God our pressing wants as though in response to a great general need. This too is possible and natural, and it belongs to the most powerful religious experiences that a man can have: the united appearance before him from whom everything comes and to whom everything returns. What happens in Holy Mass, however, is different. The Mass is not the immediate expression of an existence capable of understanding and redeeming itself spiritually. It is not a creation of that power which shaped the word of praise and the revelatory act from the emotion of the hour but something long since independently arranged, ordered, and declared valid once and forever. It does not arise each time from the individual's or the congregation's relation to God but descends from God to the believer, demanding that he acknowledge it, entrust himself to it, and *do* it. It owes its existence not to Christian creativeness but to Christ's institution.

Consequently, the Mass cannot be celebrated by anyone, but only by one who is authorized. When the father is still the recognized head of the family (also its spiritual head), he can institute a custom or a celebration that becomes binding for the family. Likewise the bearer of a religious office, the priest, or (if he has spiritual authority) the king can institute a religious celebration for a certain diocese or kingdom. Religious history has countless illustrations of this. But the institution that concerns us here is valid not only for a family or a race or an empire but claims to be the absolute norm of religious celebration, as well as the heart of spiritual life for all peoples and for all ages. No human being has the power to set up such a statute. No earthly authority having such absolute power could exist, not even with the reservation that all genuine power comes from God. God never empowered any human being to institute an act obligatory for all peoples and ages. This does not mean that he could not have done so, but simply that he did not. He who did establish the unique universal institution of the Mass was no mere messenger of God, no prophet, high priest, or king but the Son of the eternal Father, God incarnate in history, who could say of himself: "All power in heaven and on earth has been given to me" (Mt 28:18). It is he who proclaims the saving truth to all men and to all ages: not as the prophets proclaimed it, "Thus speaketh the Lord," but, "I say to you" (See Mt 5:21–28, where the difference is accentuated again and again). He does not even say "My Father speaks to you through me," but "I myself say. . . ." And he adds: "Heaven and earth will pass away, but my words will not pass away" (Mt 24:35). "Go into the world and preach the gospel to every creature. He who believes and is baptized shall be saved, but he who does not believe shall be condemned" (Mk 16:15–16). At the close of the Sermon on the Mount, Jesus declares that obedience to his words is the sole basis on which life capable of existing in eternity can be founded; all life founded on anything else will disintegrate under God's gaze. (See the parable of the house built upon the sand in Mt 7:24–27.)

The miracles are worked without excitement or display; Jesus' calm, self-understood attitude toward them is that of one accustomed to doing whatever he wills. Everywhere in the Old Testament God's self-revelation is sustained by his awareness that he is the Lord—not only over things but independently of things, in his own right because he is who he is. Sovereignty is elemental to him, and this same sovereignty is in Christ. Not for nothing was the name reserved solely for God immediately applied to the Son: *Kyrios Christos*. It appeared with the ease of a foregone conclusion, of necessity, since he actually was the Lord, whose sovereignty covers not only material reality but also that which is immeasurably greater: the law and the covenant. When the Pharisees protest that Jesus' disciples are breaking the law by plucking ears of grain on the Sabbath, he replies: "The Son of Man is Lord even of the Sabbath" (Mt 12:8) and with the Sabbath, the entire law. At the Last Supper he formally declares the old covenant fulfilled and he proceeds to establish the new heart and mainspring of religious life—the Eucharist (see Lk 22:20).

We know exactly when and how he went about it. The Gospels of Matthew, Mark, and Luke describe how Jesus, before his death, celebrated the Passover for the last time with his disciples. During that feast, whose celebration differed sharply from the traditional form, he instituted the new feast in his memory and the new covenant in his blood. St. John reports the speech Jesus made at Capharnaum, where he promised men his Eucharistic flesh and blood (See Jn 6). Finally, St. Paul speaks of it in the eleventh chapter of his first Epistle to the Corinthians, where he stresses the fact that the Lord himself revealed it to him.

What Jesus instituted was ratified by God. Man has here no call to create or determine; his task is to obey and act. Moreover, the institution itself is entrusted to a special authority for protection and guidance.

It is conceivable that the Lord could have instituted the mystery and then left it to the pious inspiration of the believers. Had he done so, it would have passed through history, formed and colored by the peculiarities of various governments, races, epochs. The development of its central theme would have been handed over to the experience and creative powers of the believers. But this is not what Christ did. He did not entrust his institution to the freely streaming spirit or to the religious inspiration of the moment but to an office which he himself established. He wanted his followers to live not as a loose collection of individuals with their sundry convictions and experiences but as a constitutional unit, as a *Church.* When he chose the apostles he was already conferring office and authority upon the Church: "Amen, I say to you, whatever you bind on earth shall be bound also in heaven; and whatever you loose on earth shall be loosed also in heaven." "He who hears you, hears me; and he who rejects you, rejects me; and he who rejects me, rejects him who sent me" (Mt 18:18; Lk 10:16). That office was to continue through "all days, even unto the consummation of the world" (Mt 28:20). Consequently the apostles were to have successors to whom that office could be passed. To this office, to the Church, Christ's institution was entrusted. Her authority determines the form and details of the sacred service. Though it has adapted itself to the characteristics of peoples and periods during the course of centuries, its core has remained the same, and it is the Church that has kept it intact. The adaptations themselves sprang only partly from the differences of historical settings; the predominant cause for all modifications was the ecclesiastical office itself that, constantly active, adapted and rearranged details, yet preserved the efficacy and unity of the whole.

From this we begin to see the attitude that is required of us: faith, piety, and vital participation. These are not to be shaped and guided solely by private experience and religious creativeness nor are they to be given free rein; they are to be practiced in the spirit of acceptance and obedience. When believers attend Holy Mass, they go not to express their own religious emotion nor to receive direction and inspiration from the spiritual talents of a man who enjoys their special trust. They enter into an order established by God; they go to participate in a prescribed service.

Criticism of liturgical details may be acceptable, but no matter how well qualified we might be for fundamental criticism or for religious self-expression, in all essentials we must renounce both our private desires and our personal disapproval. This does not mean that the believer is placed under tutelage; it is simply a clarification of domains. Criticism is good where it makes sense; criticism of the Mass makes none. One can very well criticize the lighting system of a city but not the course of the sun; one can find fault with the arrangement of a particular garden but not with the natural order of growth, bloom, and fruition. Here it is a question of something similar, only incomparably greater. The Lord's institution belongs to revelation and with revelation to creation itself. To see this is to possess the key to understanding creation and to accept it is the first step toward the sanctuary.

23. THE MEMORIAL

The preceding chapter stressed the timeless, institutional nature of the Mass so essential for our understanding of it. We saw that it is no immediate (hence necessarily varying) expression of religious sentiments or needs but something permanent, arranged once and for all, that it was authorized by him who has "all power in heaven and on earth," and that it demands to be performed according to the will of its Institutor.

Now we proceed a step further, a small step, for what is at stake is so important and so rarely understood fully, that we should spare no pains to bring out the thought completely and clearly.

The institution of the Mass has one further element: it is a memorial.

"Institutions" appear everywhere in the religious life of mankind. They give freely streaming experience its permanent and binding form. The contents of that form vary greatly. They may evolve around an important turning-point in the calendar of the year, spring, for instance. Then the celebration welcomes and honors the new beginning of growth with festivities that invoke the blessing of the godhead. Or the theme may be an important turning-point in the seasons of human life. For example, the celebration of adolescence, in which the maturing youth is consecrated for the life that awaits him, his powers of fertility are sanctified, and the new adult is received into the tribal community. Whatever the motive behind the celebration, some essential life-process always receives its religious consecration. Some personality of talent and authority introduced the chief symbols, adapting and developing them to suit his particular tribe or race and making the whole obligatory for posterity.

Quite aside from the Person who instituted Holy Mass, what takes place there is of an entirely different nature. In the tribal celebration's universal values, teachings, and regulations of a nature half religious, half natural find expression: seasonal or life-rhythms, guilt and expiation, the beginning and end of war, the major visitations of drought, hunger, pestilence and the like that threaten the coming year. In the Mass we are concerned with a single Person and his destiny. What is repeatedly executed and invoked is no natural or intellectual or mysterious power-relationship common to all human existence, but the memory of One who lived once and of his destiny. Why? Not because he was a great ruler or lawgiver or warrior from the worldly point of view, an innovator of important arts or sciences but because his life and work is decisive for men's salvation; because he is the Savior.

Of course we do find other religious celebrations in which the sacred action invokes a specific religious figure of the past and represents important aspects of his destiny. In the Greek mysteries, for example, Dionysius' death at the hands of the Maenads and the resurrection of his torn body to new life; and the Demeter cult, which recalls the lament of the Earth-Mother for her lost daughter and the joy of finding her again. These festivals too dramatize a specific event. But the beings represented in the Dionysian mysteries and in those of the Demeter or Hippolytus were never historical. Their importance lay in their relation to the senses and in the powers they personified. Mythological figures personify elements of the world itself. Dionysius never really lived in a specific country, never met a historical fate. What reality he did possess was the mystery of life he represented in all its glory and danger, a mystery that prevails wherever there are living realities and which is particularly apparent at the junctures of life—spring, harvest time, and the like. Dionysius was a creation of mythical poetry. Jesus was no myth, no poetry, no symbol but reality. The distinction is fundamental, because once religious research had discovered the myths, there was a strong effort to make Christianity "another myth religion." Actually its sharp distinction from the world of myth is indisputable. Even the fact that its Founder and his apostles come to us from the land and tradition of the Old Testament precludes any blurring of the borders of reality, for the Old Testament is anything but mythical. Myths are figures and events employed by the visionary and symbol-creating genius to interpret the meaning of existence religiously. Such creative personalities lived so close to existence, were so deeply imbued with the total religious experience of a race or an age, and expressed the essence of that race or age so perfectly that their vision was authoritative for a very long time. But always it was a question of myths, not of reality, or to be more exact, not of historical reality. What is real in the myth is the implication it gives to existence, the mysterious power it expresses through the symbol of the god and his fate. Myths of this kind do not exist in the Old Testament, which is based not on a religious world-mystery as glimpsed by sacrosanct visionaries from hallowed shrines but on the simple reality of holy God, who exists independently of the world. God is not the *Urgrund* or mysterious foundation of the world but its Creator and Lord. When it so pleases him, he summons specific people, draws them into a particular relationship with himself, and imposes upon them the obligation to carry out his will. Atmosphere, attributes, spiritual attitude, decisive values and life-forms—here everything is different. Even those texts which at first glance seem to be of a mythical nature, for example, the stories of Creation and of the Flood, on closer scrutiny reveal that they have nothing to do with mythology. It is blind and profoundly dishonest to speak of the "Creation and Flood Myths" of the Old Testament. Anyone who sincerely wants to see the essential difference between the stories of Scripture and the sagas of Babylonia and other Oriental countries can. Jesus comes to us not from the shadowy realm of mythology but from the clear sunlight of the Old Testament.

Jesus is not just another personification of the spiritual power of redemption, not a savior-godhead comparable to Osiris and Dionysius. He really lived. He was the living Son of God become man. A human being. He took his place in the history of a particular country, worked in definite ascertainable areas during certain years which can, with slight variations, be historically determined. The known life of Jesus the Nazarene is undeniably unique. In all essentials his destiny and death were known and reliably reported in world history. Not even his enemies tried to dismiss him as a myth. Jesus' spot in history is not in the dim language of a Dionysius, seemingly part of a past that may be reached by turning back, but actually unattainable because it lies not in time but in the timelessness of sense and symbol. Jesus' life and Person have all the abundance of spiritual, all-redeeming strength, yet at the same time they give clear, historical answers to the questions "How?" and "When?" and "Where?" Such, then, is the Jesus commemorated in the Mass.

The establishment of his memorial did not issue from the Christ-experience of some prophet or apostle but was ordained by the Lord himself. It rose with the same historical clarity as that which it commemorates; it is even more: a part of the life of its Institutor. On the evening before his death Jesus gathered up and placed into it his entire destiny that it might be passed on to all men.

The Old Testament is neither a nature religion nor the religion of a certain race; it springs from a specific act of God that is the cornerstone of further action. The beginning of the religion of the Old Testament is the beginning of a history, the history of the covenant between God and certain men of his choosing, first with Abraham, then on Sinai with the descendants of Abraham. The event that concerns us here is similar, but it exists on an incomparably loftier and more significant plane. It enfolds Jesus' whole historical existence in one holy commemorating act which simultaneously expresses God's new relationship to men: the new covenant, founded on the act and Person of Jesus Christ. Henceforth history continues as the history of the kingdom of God among men.

Therefore, when we go to Mass, it is not to participate in a time-honored symbolical act that gives religious expression to our own existence but in order to commemorate a specific Personality, Jesus, and his destiny. This Personality is no prophetic-poetic creation; he really lived. He was born in the reign of Augustus in the year that the Roman emperor ordered a census-taking of his whole empire. He died while Pontius Pilate was the Roman procurator in Palestine. He was born in Bethlehem and raised in Nazareth. He lived, taught, and worked outwardly much like other teachers of his day. Were archeology to succeed in excavating the synagogue which existed at that time in Nazareth, we could say: Here on this spot Jesus sat when he interpreted Isaiah and the storm of fury reported in St. John broke loose against him (Jn 4).

The Mass is the commemoration of a historic reality. It is a memorial in the strictest sense of the term.

24. THE MEMORIAL OF
THE NEW COVENANT

How did Jesus establish the act by which he passed on to his followers the memorial of his Person and redemptory fate? According to St. Luke he did so as follows:

> Now the day of the Unleavened Bread came, on which the Passover had to be sacrificed. And he sent Peter and John, saying, "Go and prepare for us the Passover that we may eat it." But they said, "Where cost thou want us to prepare it?" And he said to them, "Behold, on your entering the city, there will meet you a man carrying a pitcher of water; follow him into the house into which he goes. And you shall say to the master of the house, 'The Master says to thee, "Where is the guest chamber, that I may eat the Passover there with my disciples?"' And he will show you a large upper room furnished; there make ready." And they went, and found just as he had told them; and they prepared the Passover.
> And when the hour had come, he reclined at table, and the twelve apostles with him. And he said to them, "I have greatly desired to eat this Passover with you before I suffer; for I say to you that I will eat of it no more, until it has been fulfilled in the kingdom of God." And having taken a cup, he gave thanks and said, "Take this

and share it among you; for I say to you I will not drink of the fruit
of the vine, until the kingdom of God comes."

And having taken bread, he gave thanks and broke, and gave it
to them, saying, "This is my body, which is being given for you;
do this in remembrance of me." In like manner he took also the
cup after the supper, saying, "This cup is the new covenant in my
blood, which shall be shed for you." (Lk 22:7–20)

It is the feast of the Passover, which in accordance with the law is celebrated annually before the great Easter Sabbath as a fulfillment of the divine
command recorded in the twelfth chapter of the Book of Exodus. For
centuries the Hebrews had been living in slavery in Egypt. Then God ordered Moses to command Pharaoh to liberate them. Pharaoh had refused,
and the mysterious plagues sent by God to overcome his resistance had
affected him only briefly. Now the last and most dreadful of the plagues,
designed to break his stubbornness, was at hand: the death of all the firstborn in the land, of men and of beasts. But to prove to his people that he
was the Lord and to burn the memory of the liberation deep into their
consciousness, God gave the event a form that could not fail to impress
itself on the mind and the emotions alike. He commanded every Hebrew
family to slaughter a lamb and to paint the doorposts with its blood, so
that the angel of death on his way through the land would see the sign and
pass over (see Ex 12:11–14). Not only was the memory of this event to be
kept alive by record and recollection, it was to be celebrated each year in
liturgical ceremony. Thus God instituted the feast of the Passover, or Pasch.

At first the celebration had the form of a grave memorial, but gradually
it assumed the character of a joyous festival. The meal grew increasingly
rich. Those at table no longer stood, girt for the journey and staff in hand,
but reclined comfortably; no longer did they eat in the originally prescribed
haste, but they dined in untroubled leisure.

The ritual of the feast was roughly as follows. To begin with, the host
mixed and blessed wine in a beaker, which was then passed around. Then

the first course was eaten, and the second beaker was blessed and circulated. After that the host broke the unleavened bread lying on the table and handed each guest a piece. For each he dipped a small bunch of bitter herbs into a bowl and proffered it. Now a number of psalms were recited and the lamb was consumed, followed by a third beaker and a fourth. More psalms concluded the celebration. During the meal the host described the great event that was being commemorated in such a manner that those present could imagine themselves back in the days of Moses.

Jesus broke this pattern. He, who knew himself Lord of the law and the covenant, put an end to the thought hitherto, and commemorated and established instead a new memorial. Similarly he put an end to the covenant that had been established by the event commemorated, and he sealed the new covenant of redemption with his death.

We can see the exact place where Jesus intervened. The cup mentioned by St. Luke in the foregoing passage is the third beaker of the Pasch. One interpreter beautifully complements the Lord's words, "Take this and share it among you" with "for the last time according to ancient rite." Then Jesus takes bread, offers thanks, breaks it, and gives it to them; again the act which the host had always performed, only now it receives a new significance in Jesus' accompanying words: "This is my body, which is being given for you." Whereupon he takes the cup, "after the supper," as the host had always taken it, blesses it, thanks God, and offers it—again with the new significance of his words: "This cup is the new covenant in my blood, which shall be shed for you."

The old covenant, sealed with the blood of sacrificial animals, is at an end. Now a new covenant has been sealed, again with blood—that of Christ. He himself is offered up, like the lamb they have just slaughtered and consumed: his body, "which is being given for you"; his blood, "which shall be shed for you."

Here too it is a commemoration: "do this in remembrance of me." St. Paul continues the thought in his first Epistle to the Corinthians, in which he writes: "For as often as you shall eat this bread and drink this cup, you proclaim the death of the Lord, until he comes" (11:26).

That is the event upon which the institution of the Mass rests. Christ himself, his love and his redeeming fate are its contents, which he poured into the mold of the ancient covenant, now brought to completion. Only the form remains, the ceremonial supper. Henceforth the new covenant is there to contain those contents to the end of history—"until he comes."

---

25. REALITY

At the Last Supper we saw how the Lord established institution upon institution: the memorial of his saving love and its covenant between God and the new holy people upon the memorial of the liberation from Egypt under the old covenant, now completed. For he "to whom all power" and authority has been given declares it terminated, since all that it promised and prepared for has been fulfilled. Now the new, valid, commemorative feast is there, to remain "until the Lord returns" at the end of time. Those who believe in him are to come together and "do this," to do exactly what he did on that last evening. The command involves him too; for when his followers obey and do, what happened then will happen again, just as when he himself acted. They are to take bread, give thanks, bless it and speak over it the words he spoke. They are to take the chalice and again thank, bless, and speak as he did. Not just anyone is entitled to do this, but those whom Jesus addressed at that time, his table-companions at the last Passover, the apostles, to whom he had already committed his authority (see Mt 10); after them, those to whom they in turn would pass on their powers—the bishops and their assistants in the divine office, the priests. What these bearers of office do will be no private act. The whole concept of office suggests something that lies not in the sphere of the personally creative or the spontaneous but in the law and in the delegation of authority. An office exists not for its bearer but for all, for the whole. When the priest performs what the Lord commanded, all act with him, so that after the Lord's death one can truly say that "they," the believers, "continued steadfastly in the teaching of the apostles and in the communion of the breaking of the bread and in the prayers" (Acts 2:42). "And continuing daily with one accord in the temple, and breaking bread in their houses, they took their food with gladness and simplicity of heart, praising God and being in favor with all the people" (Acts 2:46–47).

From this we see that at the time the Christians were still living in the old order, observing the prescribed services of the temple as the others did. They had not yet realized that the temple with its services, together with the entire order of the Old Testament, was ended and that a new life-pattern was slowly taking shape. Already the little community has something entirely of its own, the ceremonial breaking of bread "in their houses." In all probability, groups of early Christians met in homes large enough for the purpose. At first there was simply an ordinary meal, an expression of fraternal unity, and a means of helping the poorer among them. Sometimes however, probably on Sundays, the meal took on a special, festive note (see Acts 20:7). It was always a real meal, though judging from St. Paul's first Epistle to the Corinthians, it was not always an entirely spiritual affair! The Epistle is concerned chiefly with current abuses, but it also suggests how those gatherings were supposed to be, and how—at least in the beginning—they usually were. The believers shared together the *Agape* or meal of love and community in the sight of God, to which each contributed something. On Sundays and special days the celebration, longer and more impressive, was deeply imbued with the memory of the Lord. On those days the one who presided over the meal, the apostle or his representative, related the story of Jesus' life and teaching and salutary death. In the first Epistle to the Corinthians, for instance, we see St. Paul urging the believers not to forget that they "proclaim the death of the Lord" whenever they partake—the proclamation referring to the solemn pronouncement and praise of the sacred mysteries to follow. Here again the old Passover tradition of the host's reverent account of the exodus from Egyptian slavery is terminated and supplanted by the new message of our liberation through Jesus Christ.

Then, at a certain moment in the meal, the Lord's representative took bread and the cup, acting as the Lord had commanded him to do. Before this it has been commemoration in the spirit, a speaking and hearing, weighing and accepting. Now it is still commemoration, but of a totally different kind. For that which was commemorated during the first part of the Mass was not actually present, save in the imagination of the believers, in the continually efficacious love and grace that stirred in their hearts and souls. Now the significance of the event changes. The moment the priest, as the Lord's representative, speaks the words, "This is my body," what is "commemorated" is also actually present in truth and in reality.

"This is my body," "this is my blood"; under no circumstance may the "is" in these holiest of sentences be interpreted as "means" or "is a symbol of" my body and blood. If ever the Lord's admonition, "Let your speech be, 'Yes, yes'; 'No, no'; and whatever is beyond these comes from the evil one" was deeply urgent, it is here. It is not only wrong but sacrilegious to tamper with these words. What they express is simplest truth, and what takes place is pure reality. He who speaks them is neither a "great" nor "the greatest" religious personality of millennia but the Son of God. His words are no expression of mystical profundity but a command of him who has all earthly and heavenly power. They have no equivalent in human speech for they are words of Omnipotence. We can compare them only with other words of the Lord, when "he arose and rebuked the wind and the sea, and there came a great calm" (Mt 8:26); or, to the leper, "I will, be thou made clean" (Mt 8:3); or to Jairus's dead child, "Girl, arise!" (Lk 8:54). Their real equivalent is the Father's "Be" (light made) from which creation itself emerged. (See the first chapter of Genesis.) Christ gave these sacred words to those he delegated to guard and execute his memorial. Their origin does not lie in the priest or bishop who speaks them but in Christ, who gave them to priest and bishop. Yet because they are God-given (given entirely) through grace, they become the priest's own words when he speaks them in obedience to Christ. Hence the Mass is a commemoration, but a commemoration of a very special kind. By the words of the Transubstantiation, what took place on Maundy Thursday, Christ's gift of self as nourishment for eternal life, takes place again—in a form that also outwardly resembles the Savior's act on that holy night.

The commemoration of the Mass is unique. Since it does not exist at all on the human level, it is impossible to judge it from here, or to "compare" it with other apparently similar religio-symbolic acts. Who are we to define the limits of its possibilities? All we can do is to "hear," for what is taking place is revelation. And it could not be revealed more simply or directly; there can be no question of symbolism here. The apostles were no modern psychologists or symbolists, but men of antiquity, whose thinking was characteristically objective and realistic. They had not forgotten the great speech at Capharnaum in which Jesus had insisted (for many to the point of intolerability) on the fact that he was to offer himself as real food and real drink, thus forcing his followers to an uncompromising either-or of faith. There is not a trace of symbolism in the Acts of the Apostles, in the First Epistle to the Corinthians, or in any of the earliest Christian writing on this sacred mystery. Without exception it is taken as revelation, which we cannot call into question, asking whether it be possible. It is a communication and a command of God, for whom all things are possible. Our attitude can be neither that of testing nor of criticizing; it can only be that of belief, and belief implies obedience. As it is a question of mystery, we must acknowledge it solely because of God's Word. As soon as we lose sight of this fact, everything is lost. That is why there is the call of warning and reminding just prior to the heart of the Mass, the Consecration: the call *mysterium fidei*. Don't forget: we have here a mystery of the faith!

This cry, this call reminds us of the speech at Carpharnaum, where the same possibility of rejecting salvation had been displayed:

Many of his disciples therefore, when they heard this, said, "This is a hard saying. Who can listen to it?" But Jesus, knowing in himself that his disciples were murmuring at this, said to them, "Does this scandalize you? What then if you should see the Son of Man ascending where he was before? It is the spirit that gives life; the flesh profits nothing. The words that I have spoken to you are spirit and life. But there are some among you who do not believe." For Jesus knew from the beginning who they were who did not believe, and who it was who should betray him. And he said, "This is why I have said to you, 'No one can come to me unless he is enabled to do so by my Father.'" From this time many of his disciples turned back and no longer went about with him. Jesus therefore said to the Twelve, "Do you also wish to go away?" Simon Peter therefore answered, "Lord, to whom shall we go? Thou hast words of everlasting life, and we have come to believe and to know that thou art the Christ, the Son of God." (Jn 6:60–69)

26. Hour and Eternity

All human events are transitory; consequently they are precious, for they cannot be repeated. What is past is gone forever. Something else can and will take place, but the past event itself can never return. Every moment comes but once, and that is why life is ever new. Something in us is continually welcoming what is about to come and mourning what is about to go. The beauty of life is inseparable from affliction; life's riches are frighteningly impermanent. And the transitory is always brief, no matter how long it lasts. It is the opposite of eternal.

Even so-called duration, time long enough to enable something to take root, grow and fulfill itself, is only a pause in the essential flow; it is not an escape from it. Natural science teaches us that nothing in the world can be lost. Though the forms of energy and matter may change, matter and energy themselves remain; the energy consumed in any task returns in its effects. The whole system, however, exists only for an instant. We call a great work or deed "imperishable," but this is true only as long as there are men who cherish and perpetuate it. We all have the feeling that a genuine imperishableness must exist somewhere, but this is only a vague intuition, a "claim" on existence, a hope of some mysterious realm in which all that has achieved validity is preserved forever. The feeling becomes clearer and more tangible only when we relate that realm to God, who receives all that is valid into his eternity. But the uneasy question remains: Is what man considers valid really so, even before God?

How was it with the Son of Man? In one way the transient quality of Jesus' life seems particularly and painfully evident, for not only did that life come to an end, as does all human life, but its unutterably divine costliness was prematurely demolished by a will so evil and so destructive that we never cease to wonder how this was possible. But there was something more about Jesus; not only the fact that his life, with every step he took, penetrated ever more deeply into the already perfect, the already immortal. We act upon decisions of the spirit, which is immortal and hence already has something of eternity about it. The decision itself, however, begins and ends in time. With Jesus it was different. Not only was his will spiritual, it was permeated by the divine will of the eternal Son of God. Thus even his decisions had an underlying depth which reached from the gesture of his hand to the divine resolution. They were no longer temporal but eternal. Jesus' acts began, unfolded, and ended in time, but both the resolve from which they sprang and the power by which they were sustained were eternal. In brief, everything the Lord did took place in time but came from eternity; and since eternity is unchangeable, everything he did was immortal.

This is a great and impenetrable mystery. Earthly things are buried in transitoriness, and for us eternity is still only a hope. We are unable to bridge the two. God alone makes this possible through what Scripture calls "the new creation": transfiguration. The temporal is not erased but assumed into eternity, there to acquire a quality for which we now have no concept. One day, though, our whole thinking, now locked in earthly transitoriness, will receive that liberating quality, and we shall be given along with the "new heaven and the new earth" the new eye, which really sees, and "the mind of the Lord" (1 Cor 2:16).

This mode of being and seeing was Jesus', with whom it came into existence. He brought it to us and in such a way that we might share in it. He is "the new," the "beginning." As long as he lived on earth that beginning remained veiled, but it was already here. He had to bear earthly bondage and transitoriness through to the end, because he had become "like us in all things" in order to expiate our sins. It was not until the Resurrection that the new was able to break through.

After the mysterious forty days in which, disregarding the laws of nature, he appeared and disappeared at will, seeming to hesitate incomprehensibly between time and eternity, he returned to the Father and is now completely eternal. There was a heresy which attempted to free the Son of God from the "taint" of earthliness by teaching that he left his body and everything connected with it here below and returned to "pure" divinity. Unfortunately, this teaching destroys the essence of all that is Christian. The Son of the eternal Father became man in divine earnestness, which means irrevocably. Hence he remains man in all eternity. To be a man means to have a body, not an idealized, general sort of body, but one's own specific body. This is what St. John means when he writes in his first epistle, "I write of what was from the beginning, what we have heard, what we have seen with our eyes, what we have looked upon and our hands have handled: of the Word of Life. And the Life was made known and we have seen, and now testify and announce to you, the Life Eternal which was with the Father, and has appeared to us . . . in order that you also may have fellowship with us, and that our fellowship may be with the Father, and with his Son Jesus Christ" (Jn 1:1–3). The "Life" or "body" "our hands have handled" is not only the impassive form but also gesture, deed, suffering, and destiny. Everything that happened to the Lord is evident in his resurrected "body." Scripture bears staggering witness to this fact in John's report of its wounds, so corporal and deep that the incredulous Thomas was able to obey Christ's command and put his hand "into my side" (Jn 20:27). These wounds are the banners of Jesus' life and fate, eternally received into his most vital being.

In that life nothing could be lost, for nothing took place that did not come from the everlastingness of that will with which the Son carried out the Father's decree in an historical, temporary act. Christ's entire life belongs to eternity. Two images express its imperishableness. The first appears in the deacon Stephen's great testimonial speech before the Sanhedrin: "But he, being full of the Holy Spirit, looked up to heaven and saw the glory of God, and Jesus standing at the right hand of God; and he said, 'Behold, I see the heavens opened, and the Son of Man standing at the right hand of God'" (Acts 7:55–56). It is also to be found in Mark (16:19) in the form in which it was later incorporated into the *Credo*: "sits at the right hand of God." The other image appears in the Epistle to the Hebrews, in the powerful passage in which Jesus, the true High Priest, strides through the courtyards of time across the threshold of death into eternity's holy of holies, bearing the sacrificial blood offering of the New Testament before the majesty of the Father, in order to reconcile his justice.

In the light of these remarks on time and eternity what does the commemoration with which Jesus entrusted his followers signify?

We are not going to try to understand now the relation between God's eternal life and events in time. The attempt would only result in a confusion of both concepts. One day we shall be able to understand—when we have been endowed with "the new," with that comprehension of the resurrected life which is the gift of grace. Now we can but sense the mystery of redeemed existence, feeling our way toward it with lowered eyes. In this world, God's decree is fulfilled in the succession of temporal events; but God himself is eternal—He always was and always will be. God realizes himself both in universal space and in specific space or locality; he exists, however, in the pure here and now. He manifests himself in the differentiation of forms, relationships, characteristics; yet he himself is of an undivided Oneness. Hence every hour with its content brushes God's eternity; every place with its content touches divine omnipresence; every form and every characteristic finds itself again in his all-inclusive simplicity.

And what is true of God is true also of him who sits on the Father's right, Christ. His earthly life has been assimilated into eternity, henceforth to be linked irrevocably to every earthly hour redeemed by his destiny. The Lord's earthly life is directly applicable to everyone he loves, to every place, and in every situation. Wherever a man believes in Christ, he finds himself in direct contact with him—and not only with the Son of God, but with the God-man in all the abundance of His redemptory existence on earth. St. Paul says that in every believer an unfathomable mystery unfolds: Christ "above" who "sitteth at the right hand of God" (Col 3:1) is simultaneously "below" and "within" that believer. In all the richness of its salutary destiny, Jesus' life—his childhood, maturity, suffering, dying, and resurrection—unwinds anew in every Christian, thus forming his real and everlasting existence (Eph 4:13). "It is now no longer I that live, but Christ lives in me" (Gal 2:20).

What happens in a general manner whenever a person believes in the Lord, whenever Christ's redemptive life becomes that person's existence, takes place in a special, specific form in the commemoration which Jesus himself established. The instant Christ's representative speaks his words over the bread and wine, Christ steps from eternity into place and hour, to become vitally present with the fullness of his redemptory power in the form of the particular, created species of bread and wine. There is no approach to this sacred procedure from our earthly experience. We can say neither that it is possible nor that it is impossible. We can only accept it as God's "mystery of faith," this truth that is the beginning of all beginning. It is the truth by which a man is summoned, which he obeys, to which he entrusts himself, and from which his thinking takes its new point of departure. Once given and accepted, this beginning becomes the key to infinite realms.

When the intellect attempts to pin down this truth in concepts or to express it in words, it becomes very difficult. But is it in itself so difficult? Words do not seem to hit the mark. Actually it is not difficult but

mysterious, though it can become difficult—in the sense of the listeners at
Capharnaum, who rejected Jesus' revelation: "This is a hard saying. Who
can listen to it?" (Jn 6:60). Such difficulty is a question of the heart's revolt
against the new beginning, of the self-confinement of the world, shutting
itself off from the true light (Jn 1:5–11). Once a person honestly desires
understanding, he senses the truth without being able to express it. And
again we turn to the example of Capharnaum: "This is why I have said to
you, 'No one can come to me unless he is enabled to do so by my Father.'
From this time many of his disciples turned back and no longer went about
with him. Jesus therefore said to the Twelve, 'Do you also wish to go away?'
Simon Peter therefore answered, 'Lord, to whom shall we go? Thou hast
words of everlasting life, and we have come to believe and to know that
thou art the Christ, the Son of God.'" This is the rescuing act: we do not
understand, but we believe. The words "mystery of faith" have a double
significance. They warn: Beware of trying to judge with human values as
your intellectual criteria! But they also invite: Believe your redeemed hearts,
which feel the superabundance of the truth that saves!

27. Mimicry or Liturgical Form

Holy Mass is the commemoration of the Person and redemptory destiny of Christ.

There are various forms of commemoration. One is that of the monument, a constant reminder to forgetful men of something that has been. This great form of commemoration is used chiefly to stimulate the national or ethnic memory. Rarer, but also impressive, is the memorial in which something transitory by nature is given "permanent form" through the continuation of its action; for instance, the memorial flame, which, carefully guarded in some sanctuary, burns unceasingly. Essentially something that expires quickly, flame is the symbol *par excellence* of the self-consuming. Here its natural action is brought to a "standstill," remaining just active enough to attract the attention and stir the mind. Water may be used similarly, the play and rustle of a fountain acting as a perpetual reminder of something past but unforgotten, a symbol of unstinted generous service. Whatever form it takes, a commemoration of this kind has the basic characteristic of something continuous, unchanging, that steadily holds its ground in the passing flow of life with all its haste and inconstancy.

It would be perfectly possible to commemorate the Lord in this fashion. Indeed, it is often done, for example, on a mountain peak or at some other significant spot where a cross has been erected. There the cross is not only a sacred image, but it is also a monument. But in the Mass it is different. The memorial that Christ established is commemorated in the form of an action that itself commemorates an event or series of events: the life, death, and resurrection of the Savior. To be rendered present—not only as an act of the mind or heart, but in its own full reality—this event must be represented in the form of an action which begins, unfolds, and ends. Into this passing act, so perfectly expressive of our own fleeting existence, steps the eternal. Thus all that exists in absolute permanence in God is packed into the brief span of an earthly event.

The believer's participation is likewise an act. Not a mere beholding and adoring but a cooperation. However inviolable from the standpoint of Christian teaching the adoration of the Eucharist is, and however fundamental and necessary the clear position it holds against error, there is a danger of its forcing the basic, active nature of the Lord's memorial into the background of the believers' consciousness. When the host is exposed for adoration, it gives an impression of permanence quite opposed to the act of Jesus' commemoration, into which the believer is meant to enter and in which he should actively participate. In what form does this sacred act take place?

It would be natural enough to take Christ's command to "do this" literally, even in the external sense and simply imitate what the Lord did on Maundy Thursday. Countless examples of commemorative folk-customs and festivals the world over testify to man's fondness for dramatization of historical events. Christian thought too has expressed itself dramatically time and again. We have only to consider the age-old devotion of the Way of the Cross, originally practiced in Jerusalem itself, where Christians piously retraced the actual path Christ took from Pilate's praetorium to Golgotha. Jesus' bequest that the Last Supper and his imminent death be commemorated could easily have led to the perpetration of the communal meal in its original form, the *Agape*, the meal of brotherly love immediately followed by the celebration of the Eucharist. In this form it actually was celebrated for quite a long time. However, abuses cropped up very soon, and to judge from the sharpness of St. Paul's criticism, they must have been grave:

> So then when you meet together, it is no longer possible to eat the Lord's Supper. For at the meal, each one takes first his own supper, and one is hungry, and another drinks overmuch. Or do you despise the church of God and put to l shame the needy? What am I to say to you? Am I to commend you? In this I do not commend you . . . For as often as you shall eat this bread and drink this cup, you proclaim the death of the Lord, until he comes. Therefore whoever eats this bread or drinks the cup of the Lord unworthily, will be guilty of the body and blood of the Lord. But let a man prove himself, and so let him eat of that bread and drink of the cup; for he who eats and drinks unworthily, without distinguishing the body, eats and drinks judgment to himself. This is why many among you are infirm and weak, and many sleep. (1 Cor 11:20–22, 26–30)

The oft-quoted words about eating and drinking judgment do not refer, as they are frequently thought to, to the wrong done by those who receive the sacred food in a state of serious sin but to that attitude which makes the sacred meal the opposite of what it is meant to be: an expression of love between those linked by faith. What each believer brought was to be shared by all; anyone who preferred to eat his own food should take care that it at least would not differ conspicuously from the rest. Instead, the wealthy flaunted delicacies that embarrassed the poor; the one had too much and the other too little. Such lovelessness is the sin of unworthily eating and drinking the sacred nourishment of the Lord. Behind it lies the other wrong: emphasis on the physical nourishment obscures the central mystery of the feast. Such then, the consequences of the imitative form.

The attempt to commemorate Christ's death in the same form would have similar results. It has been tried, and still is, in the popular mysteries or Passion Plays. People think in pictures, and the depicted scene thrusts its way into the living present. The origin of the Passion Plays indicates that they are definitely religious. Often they have been founded by some religious group; to take part in them is an honor which presupposes a fitting way of life. Rehearsal and performance alike are preceded by religious services and originally bore the stamp of profound piety. Nevertheless, from the start they have carried the seed of degeneration. Quite aside from the dominant position, which the dramatic instinct quickly usurps, aside from the inevitable infiltration of pride and envy and all the evils connected with money and success, there is something in dramatization itself that offends faith's instinctive modesty. Although this negative reaction makes allowances as long as the play remains simple and genuinely pious and as long as it is produced rarely, it would consider it intolerable if the memorial which the Lord made the center of Christian life were to be commemorated regularly in this imitative form.

The memorial of the Mass is celebrated not in the form of a play but of a liturgy. The object commemorated is not imitated but translated into symbols.

The procedure is divided into several parts. The first part of the Mass consists in readings from Scripture and prayers corresponding more or less to the psalms of praise and the host's account of the Exodus at the beginning of the Passover meal. Then in the Offertory the gifts of bread and wine are prepared. This is reminiscent of the disciples' preparations for the Last Supper described in Matthew (26:17–19). Immediately after this, Jesus' institution itself is carried out: blessing, thanksgiving, and the sacred meal. The original form has vanished. No longer is there a table around which the faithful gather; in its place stands the altar, and however close architectural arrangement has permitted it, it still remains essentially separated from the believer. At the altar stands the priest; opposite him, united as a congregation, the believers. There are no bowls and pitchers or cups and plates on the altar—all these have been concentrated in paten and chalice. And even they are shaped to differentiate sharply from the customary instruments in daily use. The priest partakes of the sacred food and offers it to the believers in a manner entirely different from that of the ordinary meal. As for the food itself, its form has become so "spiritualized" that one can almost speak of the danger of its being unrecognizable as bread.

It is important really to understand this process of translation from one sphere of reality to another. It exists not only here. In man lives a soul, but the life of that soul is not of itself visible; it is unable to express itself alone. To do so, it must first become gesture, act, and word; it must translate itself into the language of the body in order for us to grasp it. Herein lies the true essence of what the German calls *Leib*—the vital unit of heart, mind, and body, as distinguishable from the mere physique. *Leib* is not only a vessel or an instrument but the visible manifestation of the soul. In Jesus this relation between body and soul reappears in sublime form. When God's Son came to us, he did not reveal himself directly as the *Logos*; he became man. Here in a man's human body lived divine reality, a reality which did not manifest itself in mysterious radiance or overwhelming power but which was translated into the body, gesture, word, and act of the man Jesus. In that man God was heard and seen, as St. John so vividly expresses it: "And the Word was made flesh, and dwelt among us. And we saw his glory—glory as of the only-begotten of the Father—full of grace and truth" (1:14).

The Mass moves along much the same line. The event which took place in the room of the Last Supper was in the form of the Passover as it was then celebrated. Jesus sat at the table, about him the members of his "household," the disciples. He took a loaf of bread, broke it, and spoke over it certain words in the language he ordinarily used and in the voice usual to him in particularly solemn moments. He handed the pieces to the guests, just as he had done earlier in the meal and during other Passover celebrations. He took the cup, also as usual, gave thanks, spoke the words of consecration, and handed it to the disciples. They ate and drank as they had always done. All this had the immediate form of daily reality, which it preserved for some time. But gradually it assumes a different form—the liturgical. Now the action loses its directness and becomes ceremonial and measured. At some points it only suggests; at others it elaborates on the essential, piously enclosing and veiling it. The bread assumes a new, special aspect; it becomes host. The cup becomes festive chalice; the table, altar. In place of the presiding master we have the delegated priest. The words spoken no longer spring from the immediate feeling and inspiration of the officiator, but are strictly prescribed.

Jesus' memorial had to assume this form if it was to remain a permanent part of the believers' Christian life. In its imitative form it could have been celebrated only very rarely; frequent repetition would have caused it to slip into the bizarre and embarrassing. In its liturgical form it can be celebrated at all times—on festive as on ordinary days—and in all situations, whether of sorrow, joy, or need. It has now become genuine daily service.

Of course, like any other characteristic form, the liturgical too has its dangers: it invites independent development according to its own laws. Then the ritualistic action threatens to stifle the actual sacrifice, and the essential can be discerned only with difficulty through a tangle of forms. Moreover, the disparity between the liturgical and the realistic forms may so far remove the principal event from ordinary existence that it loses touch with everyday life. Not infrequently these dangers have become reality; for this reason, the business of liturgical work today is to do everything possible to present the original form in its full clarity and power.

The believer is faced with an important task: that of discerning the essential in what meets his eye. In the altar he must see the table; in the priest, the head of the congregation; in the host, the bread; in the chalice, the cup. He must recognize the Eucharistic Supper in the sacred act with its strictly prescribed wording. It is not enough, however devoutly, to "keep up with" a mysterious celebration's prayers and hymns, readings and acts of consecration and offering. The believer must also follow the "translation" into symbols of everything that is taking place. When we watch a person we love, we do not merely observe his expression and gestures; we try to interpret those external manifestations of what is going on within. Here we have something similar, only greater. Speaking for himself and for his fellow apostles, St. John says: "I write of what was from the beginning, what we have heard, what we have seen with our eyes, what we have looked upon and our hands have handled: of the Word of Life. And the Life was made known and we have seen, and now testify and announce to you, the Life Eternal which was with the Father, and has appeared to us. What we have seen and have heard we announce to you, in order that you also may have fellowship with us, and that our fellowship may be with the Father, and with his Son Jesus Christ. And these things we write to you that you may rejoice, and our joy may be full" (1 Jn 1:1–4). The passage is very important. Jesus was the living "Epiphany" of the Son, and in the Son, of the Father. He himself said: "he who sees me sees also the Father. How canst thou say, 'Show us the Father'?" The reproving tone shows how essential was the point which Jesus was driving at and how self-evident it should have been. In his presence his followers should not merely reflect on God, they should behold God with the vital gaze of the new man. The liturgical action of the Mass is a formal rendering of Jesus' act of making his Father "visible."

28. Christ's Offering of Self

Two things are necessary for true understanding. The first is the ability to compare, differentiate, and discern causal relations and interdependencies. This is important, but more important is something unteachable: a certain sensibility to the essence of things. This quality has nothing to do with that watchfulness that is quick to notice a danger or an advantage; animals too have that faculty. It is equally far removed from curiosity, from eagerness to experience the unknown and the extraordinary for their own sakes. Avidness for experience is at best but a forerunner of the essential attitude; more often it is a caricature of it and renders a man as incapable of genuine enlightenment as would indifference. The real prerequisite of enlightenment is an intellectual and more than intellectual readiness to be struck and shaken by the revelatory impact of a thing, not because of any personal fear or desire, for here we are already beyond the range of intent and purpose; not for the sake of diversion, for at this level things cease to belong to "the interesting." Confronted with the hidden meaning behind some image or pattern of images, a man is moved to disclose it and to clear for it a path into the open, so that truth may come into its own.

Sensibility to the essence of things also exists, though of course in a different way: in the realm of faith. Here the "birth" of a truth, the emergence of its essence into the light and spaciousness of recognition, are made possible not by any contact of intellect with significance but by the power of God's light and grace. The object does not step from the world to confront the mind capable of discovering it; it does not exist in itself at all (in the manner of earthly objects, which can be grasped, plumbed, and exploited by exhaustive study); it exists only in God and must be "given," revealed by the divine word and received by faith. It always remains a mystery that transcends the created mind. Revealed truth is neither a continuation nor a new dimension of earthly truth but something that completely overthrows earthly truth. And not only does it overthrow it, it brands it as untruth. When a man accepts divine truth in the obedience of faith, he is forced to rethink human truth. The conversion he must make embraces his whole conception of the universe, which he must conceive anew in its entirety. His readiness to do so is the measure of his enlightenment. Yet in all this upheaval his natural reason stands firm, for the *Logos* who speaks in revelation is the same *Logos* who created the universe. Thus the depth of a man's true knowledge depends upon the impact of the divine knowledge he has received. The point that is "struck" lies much deeper than mere intellectual readiness for truth: somewhere in the inmost depths of new birth and the new man.

Revelation presents twentieth-century believers with a special difficulty. We are latecomers. Our generation has heard the sacred tidings time and time again. Moreover, we live in an age that is constantly reading and writing and talking and hearing. There is such a continuous turnover of words that our "coinage" is worn smooth and thin; its stamp has grown blurred. Instead of truth we have truth's caricatures; instead of knowledge, the illusion of already knowing. Only with great effort can we free ourselves from illusory knowledge to pause, look up, and passionately inquire into the clear-cut, genuine truth of things. Are we then doomed to become incapable of possessing divine truth? Certainly not, for truth is meant for all ages; however, we must recognize and apply ourselves to this century's particular barriers to truth if we wish to clear them. Above all, we must relearn composure, meditation, and absorption—precisely the things that the different chapters of this book have attempted to describe. We must break the strings of habit, must rid ourselves of fateful seeming-knowledge, and we must remint our words so that they may again speak clearly, truthfully.

The Lord's memorial is the central mystery of our Christian life. It has taken the form of a meal at which he offers himself as the food. We were taught this in the Communion instruction of our childhood; we hear it repeated again and again in sermons and retreats; we read it in religious books. Yet are we really aware of the stupendousness of the thought?

It must have been important to the Lord that his hearers were conscious of it, for when he proclaimed the establishment of the mystery he stressed the enormity of it in a manner that could not have been accidental. His words at Capharnaum sound quite different from those of the actual establishment, where they are frugal and calm. During the tremendous act that took place on Maundy Thursday, he no longer dwells on its tremendous significance. The great test of faith has already taken place; the decision has fallen, and those who hear him now have already proved themselves. For at Capharnaum Jesus so drastically confronted his hearers with the otherness of the divine that they were not only struck but struck down. The report reads: "I am the bread of life. He who comes to me shall not hunger, and he who believes in me shall never thirst" (Jn 6:35). The Jews "murmured about him because he had said, 'I am the bread that has come down from heaven.' And they kept saying, 'Is this not Jesus the son of Joseph, whose father and mother we know? How, then, does he say, "I have come down from heaven"?'" (Jn 6:41–42).

The protest is directed not at the mystery of the Eucharist, which has not yet been proclaimed but at Jesus' claim to be, in person, the bread of faith, eternal truth. What does the Lord do? He does not mitigate what he has said; he does not attempt to explain by pointing out his place in the sacred prophecies. He goes still further, pressing the sharp point of the blade home. "I am the bread of life. Your fathers ate the manna in the desert, and have died. This is the bread that comes down from heaven, so that if anyone eats of it he will not die. . . . If anyone eats of this bread he shall live forever." Now they feel the full shock of the blow: "and the bread that I will give is my flesh for the life of the world" (Jn 6:48–52). It would seem to be high time to modify these words, or at least to explain them. Instead of coming to the rescue of his floundering hearers Jesus adds: "Amen, amen, I say to you, unless you eat the flesh of the Son of Man, and drink his blood, you shall not have life in you. He who eats my flesh and drinks my blood has life everlasting and I will raise him up on the last day. For my flesh is food indeed, and my blood is drink indeed. He who eats my flesh, and drinks my blood, abides in me and I in him" (Jn 6:53–57). At this the first split runs through the group of disciples: "Many of his disciples therefore said, 'This is a hard saying. Who can listen to it?'" (Jn 6:61). Jesus' closest followers are hard-pressed, but he does not help them. He forces them to a decision of life or death: are they ready to accept the fullness of revelation, which necessarily overthrows earthly wisdom, or do they insist on judging revelation, delimiting its "possibilities" from their own perspective? "Does this scandalize you? What then if you should see the Son of Man ascending where he was before? It is the spirit that gives life; the flesh profits nothing. The words that I have spoken to you are spirit and life. But there are some among you who do not believe" (Jn 6:62–65). "The Jews" who first "murmured" against Jesus have already dispersed. Now also "many of his disciples" leave him. Jesus turns to the remaining hard core: "Do you also wish to go away?" (Jn 6:68). Still not a word of help, only the hard, pure demand for a decision. Peter replies: "Lord, to whom shall we go? Thou hast words of everlasting life, and we have come to believe and to know that thou art the Christ, the Son of God" (Jn 6:68–70). They do not understand either, but struck by the power of the mystery, they surrender themselves to it. They are dumbfounded but trustful—at least most of them. Not all, as we see from Jesus' reply: "'Have I not chosen you, the Twelve? Yet one of you is a devil.' Now he was speaking of Judas

Iscariot, the son of Simon; for he it was, though one of the Twelve, who was to betray him" (70–71).

It was to such rigorously tested men that Jesus entrusted the mystery of the Holy Eucharist; it was they who at the Last Supper first received the sacred nourishment.

Apparently there is no genuine belief without battle. Every believer worthy of the name must sometime undergo the danger of scandal and its trial by fire. Some, the intrinsically shielded children of God, are enabled to come through; certainly not the majority. We too must have felt the enormity of what took place at Capharnaum, of that which so incensed the Jews and so shocked many of the disciples that they declared Jesus' words intolerable and left him. It was the shock that probably shattered Judas' faith, the other eleven saving themselves only by a blind leap of trust to the Master's feet. The impact of the message of Capharnaum by no means leaves an impression of idyllic and sentimental wonderment, as the average book of devotions suggests. It is an unheard-of challenge flung not only at the mind but, as we see from the stark scene at Capharnaum, at the heart as well. There stands Christ and declares that he desires to give himself to us, to become the content and power of our lives. How can one person give himself to another—not things that he possesses, or knowledge or experience or help or trust or respect or love or even community of life—but his body and his soul to be our food and drink! And he means it really, not "spiritually." The quotation on which the Symbolists base their theory: "It is the spirit that gives life; the flesh profits nothing" (Jn 6:63) by no means indicates that Jesus' words over the bread and wine were intended to mean: "My spirit shall fill you; my strength shall strengthen you." He might have said this, but he did not. The whole point of the speech at Capharnaum is its insistence on real flesh, real blood, real eating and drinking—"in the spirit" of course, but that means in the Holy Spirit. The Lord was referring to sacrifice, yes, but not as the hearers' familiarity with temple sacrifice would suggest; not in the general, impersonal sense of the Old Testament, but in the intimate mystery of faith. The glorious reality of Jesus' sacrifice compares with the disciples' dim conception of it as the risen body of the Lord in the full power of the Holy Spirit with the body that stands before them.

Nothing helps but to warn ourselves: Here is the steepest, highest pinnacle of our faith (or the narrowest, most precipitous pass through which that faith must labor if it is to reach full, essential freedom). Experience has shown that those who water down reality here at the summit of Christianity continue to do so all the way down the line: in their conceptions of the Church, of the Incarnation, of Christ's divine Sonship, of the truth of the triune God. The test of Capharnaum is in truth faith's supreme test. The man who refuses to master his feelings when they stand between him and God is unfit for the kingdom of God. This is where the great conversion, the change of measuring-rods takes place. Not until the earnestness of the decision has been felt and the danger of scandal faced and overcome, does the miracle of this ultimate mystery unfold. Then, suddenly, as if self-understood, comes the blissful knowledge that love perfectly fulfilled *can* give not only all it has, but all it is: itself. No earthly love is ever perfectly fulfilled. To love in the earthly sense really means to strive for the impossible. St. John gives us the clue to the otherness of divine love: not only does God love, God is lover and he alone not only desires to love but can love "to the end" (Jn 13:1).

Jesus desires that men receive and make their own the gift of his vital essence, strength, his very Person as fully and intimately as they receive and assimilate the strength and nourishment of bread and wine. He even adds that the person who is not so nourished cannot possess ultimate life. No earthly gift of love, even if it were possible, could ever be the perfect gift that Jesus' self-offering is—utterly devoid of accompanying impurities and toxins. He is total purity, total power, total vitality and more: the prerequisite of that immortal, ultimate life which alone is capable of existence before God throughout eternity. Jesus really means what he said at the Last Supper: "Thomas said to him, 'Lord, we do not know where thou art going, and how can we know the way?' Jesus said to him, 'I am the way, and the truth, and the life'" (Jn 14:6).

29. Encounter and Feast

The participant in Holy Mass enters into a community at table. Early in the Mass he receives God's word, which he accompanies with his prayers, glorifying God and placing his personal concerns at the feet of the provident Father. Then, beholding and participating, he helps to prepare the sacred meal to which he brings his offering. And however impersonal the money-piece, it is the accepted substitute for the more vital form of giving. Now with the priest he turns to the Father and receives through faith the presence of him who said: "I am the living bread that has come down from heaven" (Jn 6:52). At Communion he sees in spirit the Father's hand proffering the sacred nourishment, which he reverently accepts, that he may "have life." But this conception of the Lord's Supper or Feast does not stand alone. It is coupled with another: that of Christ's "coming."

Spiritual language has its own idiom for this second aspect, which it expresses with great simplicity. Everywhere we meet sentences such as these: Christ is present in the Mass; in Communion the Lord gives himself to the communicant; he lingers with him. Those who insist that spiritual language is sometimes faulty, and who should on this point be soberly corrected, should re-read the text of Christ's speech at Capharnaum. Referring to the promised Eucharist, the Lord himself uses the image of a coming, an encounter. Along with his insistence on the real eating and drinking of the real food, we find such sentences as: "For the bread of God is that which comes down from heaven and gives life to the world." "Not that anyone has seen the Father except him who is from God, he has seen the Father." "I am the living bread that has come down from heaven. If anyone eats of this bread he shall live forever; and the bread that I will give is my flesh for the life of the world." "As the living Father has sent me, and as I live because of the Father, so he who eats me, he also shall live because of me" (see Jn 6:33–57).

The "meat indeed" and "drink indeed" offered by the hand of the Father is not a thing but a Person; not "it" but he, the supreme Person praised in all eternity. Hence the reverent believer is naturally inclined to feel that the words about eating and drinking somehow debase the sacred Person of Christ. St. John is the Evangelist who had to wage an endless battle against the heresies that began to crop up even in his lifetime. That is why his wording of the truth in all fundamental passages is extremely sharp. In his Prologue he does not state that God's Son became man, but he uses the more forceful expression: "the Word was made flesh." In reference to the Eucharist he does not use the statement employed by the Synoptics: "take and eat, this is my body," but, "He who eats my flesh and drinks my blood has life everlasting. . . . For my flesh is food indeed, and my blood is drink indeed. He who eats my flesh and drinks my blood, abides in me and I in him" (Jn 6:54–56). Here is the ultimate clarification to which a man must speak his clear, decisive "Yes!" or "No!"

It is at this point that the difficulty we mentioned becomes apparent, a genuine difficulty quite different from the stubborn contrariness of "the Jews," of the "many disciples," or of Judas at Capharnaum; here we have the valid fear that the Lord's self-offering could be dragged from the purity of his relation to us as a Person to the level of a mere thing or object. A person, and least of all he, the Holy One and Lord, cannot simply be given and taken and had; a person is not something to be passed about here and there. A person is not passed about; he comes, enters into a vital you-me relationship, and gives himself freely and personally. This is the second concept inherent in the Mass. The first was the meal; the second is the encounter. Both are expressed time and again by Christ himself as well as by the general spiritual phrases his words have inspired. The one image is sustained by words like "the true bread," the "food and drink," the "flesh for the life of the world"; the other by "come down from heaven," "He who comes to me," and by the countless expressions of the Lord's being among us, with us, his inclining lovingly toward us, his dwelling in us, and uniting himself with us.

The Mass is the Lord's memorial. We have tried to understand the word as richly and profoundly as possible; now we must go a step further. A *memorial* can commemorate only a person, not an earthquake or a particularly fruitful harvest. These can only be remembered. I can commemorate some beloved victim of the catastrophe or a loved one's joy over a blessed autumn's abundance. Commemoration always implies a person, and it presupposes a vital relationship to that person. Genuine commemoration is a projection of an already existing "we-relationship."

This is precisely what we have in Holy Mass. The memorial the Lord bequeathed us is not merely the memory of an event or the portrayal of a great figure; it is the fulfillment of our personal relation to Christ, of the believer to his Redeemer. In the Mass Christ comes in all his personal reality, bearing his salutary destiny. He comes not to just anyone, but to his own. Here again St. John brings this mystery into particularly sharp focus. God's Son comes from heaven, from the Father, whom he alone knows. He lives from the Father's vitality; everything he has and is, he has and is through the Father. But this intimate bond of love does not stop there. The Father sends his Son to men in order that he may pass on to them the divine life he has received. "As the living Father has sent me, and as I live because of the Father, so he who eats me, he also shall live because of me" (Jn 6:58).

When he became man, Jesus bridged the gulf between heaven and earth, between the Father and us once and for all. Henceforth he "is" with us in the sense that he belongs to us, is "on our side"—"Emmanuel," the

God-who-has-come. Yet in the special manner of the mystery, the Lord spans that gulf anew every time his memorial is celebrated. First, in the readings of the day, we receive word of him. Then the offerings are prepared and there is a pause. By Consecration he comes to us, the subject of an incomprehensibly dynamic "memorial," and gives us his grace-abounding attention. In Communion he approaches each of us individually and says: "Behold, I stand at the door and knock" (Rv 3:20). Insofar as the "door" swings open in genuine faith and love, he enters and gives himself to the believer for his own.

This might be the place to mention the general significance of the Lord's coming in the liturgy. What are the Christian implications of the word "feast"? When we stop to consider such things, we must remember that our century has lost touch with certain ultimate mysteries. We are rationalists and psychologists and reduce everything to the intellect or moral plane or to the subjective level of "experience." When asked what a feast is—Easter, for example, we should probably reply something to the effect that Easter is the day on which we commemorate the Resurrection of Jesus Christ, that we joyfully praise God, that filled with faith and love, and hopeful of sharing in the graces of his Resurrection, we seek out the Lord, firmly resolving to live the new life he has made available to us.

Have we expressed the essence of Easter? Not yet, for we have not touched the reality that lies at its core, the unique manner in which the Lord's Resurrection is renewed—not as a mere repetition but so that he actually steps anew from eternity into our time, our presence. (Recall what was said in the chapter "Time and Eternity.") And he comes in the pleni-tude of his whole redemptory life—each time in the particular mystery of the day that the unrolling liturgical year is commemorating: the mystery of God's Incarnation, or his Epiphany, or his Passion, or his Resurrection and Ascension. He comes to us from the Father in the power of the Holy Spirit.

To wait for him, to invite him, to go to receive and honor and praise him, to be with him, drawn into the intimacy of Communion with him—that is the Christian feast.

We begin to see how closely interwoven the concepts of the feast and the encounter are. They do not conflict, but mutually sustain each other. Each prevents the other from one-sidedness and falsehood. The concept of the coming, the encounter, guards the dignity of the person and protects the concept of the Supper from unseemliness and irreverence. It reminds us that Communion is not possession but exchange, like the reciprocal gaze of any genuine "we." On the other hand, the concept of the Supper projects that of the encounter to the incomprehensible holy mystery of ultimate intimacy. Among human beings an encounter is always relative; it never completely embraces the other person. This last unbridgeable separation is the exigency of all created love. In Holy Communion the last vestige of distance is removed, and we are assured of an "arrival" that surpasses all created possibility, genuine union.

If we wish to read more about the life that flows to us from this mystery, we should turn to the letters of the Apostle Paul. The man who writes in the Epistle to the Galatians: "It is now no longer I that live, but Christ lives in me" is the evangelist of the totally "encountered" Christ, the "Christ in us."

In the preceding chapter we concluded that participation in Holy Mass demands that we make our concept of the meal, the feast, a living one. Now we must add that participation in the Mass also consists in our awareness of our encounter with Christ, in the consciousness that he is about to come, is here in this room, is turning to me, is here! We must listen for and hear his knock on the door; we must profoundly experience his arrival and visit—without sentimentality or super-exaltation but simply, calmly, in a faith that is all truth.

30. TRUTH AND THE EUCHARIST

The action of the Lord's memorial embraces several different but inseparable concepts. We have already discussed two: that of the meal and that of Christ's coming or our encounter with him. The Father offers the believer the vital being of his Son—"the true bread." From the same Father, Christ steps into the congregation that is commemorating him and lovingly approaches each member. These are the concepts that determine the act of Holy Communion. The creature in us longs to be nourished by the abundant reality of the God-man who said: "I am the life"; the person in us watches, waits, hurries to meet the coming One, remains with him in the union of love and obedience. Behind both concepts, giving them their sacred significance, stands the tremendous fact of the redemptory sacrifice.

And still we have not touched bottom. One more thought belongs here: revelation and the pious recognition of divine truth. What does community with another person mean? Above all, it demands genuine mutual exchange, respect for his person, trust, loyalty, that simultaneous unity and reverence known as friendship or comradeship or love. Such an alliance surpasses the merely physical or merely spiritual. Because it rests on the will, it is capable of surviving the adversities to which all living things are exposed. But community has yet another element: the sharing of one another's power, radiance, and vital depths; the ability to experience with the immediacy of sympathy and love the life of the other. These elements of community are essential and irreplaceable, but alone they still do not suffice. The relationship founded on them alone would have a blind spot. Between myself and the other there must also be truth. His essence must be conveyed to me. I must appreciate his uniqueness, his attitude to life, his work and destiny. I must consent to his being as he is and make room for him, as he is, in my life. And I must know myself confirmed and accepted by him. Then our relations will be complete—not before.

The whole point of the Lord's memorial is such *communio*.

No more complete communion exists than that which Christ established between himself and those who believe in him. Of course, its perfection is one-sided, for we remain locked in egotism.

The relation of the believer to his Lord is a pure I-Thou relation, just as one redeemed is related to the freedom of the children of God. The Redeemer "comes" in a particular way that embraces every conceivable degree of person-to-person encounter and mutual fulfillment; this concept continues even to the startling second concept in which the flesh and blood of him who knew himself to be "the life" is offered as nourishment for men. Both concepts are threatened: the first by an all-too-personal sentimentality and the second by the impersonal, if not inhuman-magical. History proves that both dangers have frequently become realities. Christ is not only "the Life," but he is also "the Truth." He is the incarnate *Logos*, God's Message written in flesh and blood. His self-offering is revelation; to receive him is to receive Truth.

Once again we must consult the "commentary" to the institution of the Eucharist, Jesus' speech at Capharnaum. The crowds have experienced the miracle of the loaves, and they press about him expectantly. Now, surely, the miraculous bounty of the Messianic kingdom will be poured out! Jesus says to them: "Amen, amen, I say to you, you seek me, not because you have seen signs [that reveal divine truth], but because you have eaten of the loaves and have been filled. Do not labor for the food that perishes, but for that which endures unto life everlasting, which the Son of

Man will give you" (Jn 6:26–27). The people do not understand, so Jesus speaks more clearly: "'my Father gives you tile true bread from heaven. For the bread of God is that which comes down from heaven and gives life to the world.' They said therefore to him, 'Lord, give us always this bread.' But Jesus said to them, 'I am the bread of life. He who comes to me shall not hunger, and he who believes in me shall never thirst'" (Jn 6:33–35). The "life" he speaks of is his own. The "bread" by which it is nourished is himself. But how is that bread to be given and received? "All that the Father gives to me shall come to me, and him who comes to me I will not cast out" (Jn 6:37). In other words, it will be given through living contact with him who is the Truth; on the one hand through the radiance of all he is and says and does and suffers; on the other, through our coming to him and believing and seeing. What does one see? The divine figure of the Lord, in which the abundance of the invisible world breaks through. St. John says: "The Word was made flesh, and dwelt among us. And we saw his glory—glory as of the only-begotten of the Father—full of grace and truth" (Jn 1:14). What are to take place, then, are the revelation of Truth through God and the acceptance of that sacred truth by men. Then the concept shifts. Again he says, "I am the bread of life." But he adds, "I am the living bread that has come down from heaven. If anyone eat of this bread he shall live forever; and the bread that I will give is my flesh for the life of the world" (Jn 6:48–51). This is so novel and unheard-of that scandal sets in. Hasn't he himself insisted again and again that "the bread" is his living flesh, that the eating is a true eating? Only the manner of that eating and drinking, namely, in the spirit, remains mysteriously veiled. "It is the spirit that gives life; the flesh profits nothing" (Jn 6:63). Christ has given his hearers the clue, but they refuse it.

The coherence of the speech as a whole is immeasurably important. Christ's memorial is an act of genuine sharing in his vital existence; it is not meant to be "spiritualized" or volatilized, for it is genuine eating and drinking, though in all the dignity, breadth, power, and significance of truth. To put it bluntly, Christ, offering himself as nourishment, cannot be eaten like a piece of bread that is received and become part of our own body whether we are aware of its essence or not. The Lord has just said of this act: "It is the spirit that gives life; the flesh profits nothing. The words that I have spoken to you are spirit and life." The one who offers us himself is not any parcel of reality, but the universal *Logos*. The "nourishment" of his body is eternal, holy truth, and consequently the participation in it requires recognition of that truth; otherwise it "profits nothing."

To participate in Holy Mass means to recognize Christ as the *Logos*, Creator, Redeemer. "As often as ye shall do these things, ye shall do them in remembrance of me." "Remembrance" here does not mean only: "Do this to commemorate me." It means in addition: "While doing this, think of me, of my essence, my tidings, my destiny; all these are the Truth." It is not by accident that the essential action of the Mass is preceded by the Epistle and Gospel, for each of the sacred texts is a clue to Christ's identity, is some facet of his personality or truth, some event in his life that comes forward to be understood and accepted; each is a ray of that Truth which will be present at the Consecration no longer in word but in his real existence.

It is of primary importance that we see Truth's relation to the Mass. Piety is inclined to neglect truth. Not that it shuns it or shies away from it, but it is remarkable how readily piety slides off into fantasy, sentimentality and exaggeration. Legends and devotional books offer only too frequent and devastating proof of this; unfortunately piety is inclined to lose itself in the subjective, to become musty, turgid, *unspiritual*. Divine reality is never any of these, never falsely spiritual in the sense of the vaporous, the unsubstantial. Divine reality, which is another name for truth, remains as divinely substantial as the living Jesus who walked the earth. But it must be illuminated by the spirit—the Holy Spirit.

Truth is essential to the fullness of the Mass. It is not enough to harp on the fact that the Mass is the center and content of the Christian's life. It must also be made clear how that center may be reached and that content shared. This is possible only when truth's vital relation to the Eucharist is recognized and when truth permeates the entire act of the sacred celebration.

31. THE MASS AND
THE NEW COVENANT

Among the words Jesus used to establish his memorial, there is one that
as a rule receives little notice in instruction on the Mass: the word
about the covenant. St. Matthew's Gospel reads: "All of you drink of this;
for this is the blood of the new covenant, which is being shed for many
unto the forgiveness of sins" (Mt 26:29). St. Mark's: "This is my blood of
the new covenant, which is being shed for many" (Mk 14:24). St. Luke's:
"This cup is the new covenant in my blood, which shall be shed for you"
(Lk 22:20). In St. Paul's first Epistle to the Corinthians we also find a
reference to the covenant, resembling that in Luke (1 Cor 11:25). We see
how important the idea of the covenant is to the Church in the emphasis
she places on it. At the consecration of the wine in the Canon of the Mass
we have the words: "For this is the chalice of My Blood, of the new and
eternal testament: the mystery of faith: which shall be shed for you and for
many unto the remission of sins." What exactly does this mean?

The Passover was a feast of commemoration. We have already discussed
the event it commemorated. When the rulers of Egypt remained unmoved
by Moses' threats and God's lighter plagues, stubbornly refusing to let the
Hebrew captives go, the Lord God sent them the terrible plague of the
death of all their firstborn, human as well as animal. In order that it might

be perfectly clear who was being punished, the members of each Jewish household were commanded to slaughter a lamb and daub the doorposts of the house with its blood. Thus the angel of death would pass them by, and their oppressors would be left in no doubt that they alone were meant. That evening the lamb was to be consumed by the joyfully united members of the household, and the solemn feast was to be repeated annually in commemoration of the end of Egyptian bondage. Jesus himself had celebrated the Passover each year with his disciples. But he had given the celebration a different turn by emphasizing not so much the liberation as the event following it: the sealing of the covenant of Sinai. The Book of Exodus reports:

> So Moses came and told the people all the words of the Lord, and all the judgments. And all the people answered with one voice: We will do all the words of the Lord, which he hath spoken. And Moses wrote all the words of the Lord: and rising in the morning he built an altar at the foot of the mount, and twelve titles according to the twelve tribes of Israel. And he sent young men of the children of Israel: and they offered holocausts, and sacrificed pacific victims of calves to the Lord. Then Moses took half of the blood and put it into bowls: and the rest he poured upon the altar. And taking the book of the covenant, he read it in the hearing of the people: and they said: All things that the Lord hath spoken we shall do. We will be obedient. And he took the blood and sprinkled it upon the people, and he said: This is the blood of the covenant which the Lord hath made with you concerning all these words. (Ex 24:3–8)

The parallel is obvious. The mediator on Sinai says: "This is the blood of the covenant which the Lord hath made with you . . ." Jesus says: "This is the chalice of My Blood, of the new and eternal testament . . . which shall be shed for you."

Behind the covenant of Sinai stands an earlier covenant: the one that existed between God and Abraham. It too had been sealed in blood: After the sun had set and a dark mist had risen, a lamplike fire passed between the "divisions" [of the slaughtered, sacrificial animals]. "That day God made a covenant with Abram, saying: To thy seed will I give this land, from the river of Egypt even to the great river Euphrates" (Gen 15:17–18). And still further back, in the grey beginnings of time, looms the original covenant between God and Noe, sealed after the Flood, when Noe offered sacrifice to the Lord: "and Noe built an altar unto the Lord: and taking of all cattle and fowls that were clean, offered holocausts upon the altar. And the Lord smelled a sweet savour, and said: I will no more curse the earth for the sake of man: for the imagination and thought of man's heart are prone to evil from his youth: therefore I will no more destroy every living soul as I have done. All the days of the earth, seedtime and harvest, cold and heat, summer and winter, night and day, shall not cease" (Gen 8:20–22). "Behold, I will establish my covenant with you, and with your seed after you. . . . And God said: This is the sign of the covenant which I give between me and you, and to every living soul that is with you, for perpetual generations. I will set my bow in the clouds, and it shall I be the sign of a covenant between me, and between the earth" (Gen 9:8–13).

In all these texts we find the reference to blood, often stressed again and again. This may impress us as strange or inhuman, but we do well to refrain from judging hastily by our twentieth-century reactions. Deep in the consciousness of all races lies a knowledge of the power of blood. Blood is life in its primary and most elementary form. Its flow eases tension, appeases anger, averts the lowering fate, enables life to reassume its course. How, it is impossible to say; we can only sense the truth of this. Somehow, through the flowing of blood a new beginning is made, mysteriously fortified by the sanguinary life-power. Obviously, the primitive significance of blood cannot simply be applied as it stands to revelation, for if ever anything needed redemption, it is the dark, primeval powers of blood. However, once existence has been transfigured, all things are revealed anew, and with them the power of blood. It is significant in the covenant not because it is symbolic of the glory and terror of life but because in a special way it belongs to God, the Lord of all life. The flowing of the sacrificial blood in the Old Testament is an acknowledgment of his sovereignty, signifying the opposite of what it signifies in other religious sacrifices. It is not a kind of blood-mysticism, not a release of the divinity in nature, and not a summoning of the powers of the deep. It has nothing to do with any of these. It is simply the recognition and prayerful acknowledgment that God alone is Lord!

Upon the conception of streaming blood as an expression of ultimate obedience, God places his covenant. And again we must be careful to differentiate. The word does not signify here what it does in the various religions—namely, the alliance of a divinity with a particular tribe. There it constitutes the secret vitality of the tribe, which in turn is the immediate expression of the god's reality. Thus the two are interdependent to the point of being or nonbeing: the tribe enjoys the power and protection of its god; on the other hand, the god lives from the fertility and strength of the tribe. Their unity is effected in sacrifice. Through his offerings man strengthens the vitality of his god; then, by consuming the offerings, man avails himself of his god's strength.

In the Old Testament there is not a trace of any such conception. God is not the divinity of a people or tribe because of any natural circumstance. He is not the mysterious source of its vitality and strength, but One who summons it from the freedom of divine decree. Certainly not because he needs human expression of his existence and a steady stream of earthly vitality in order to exist. He needs neither the Hebrew people nor any other people, for he is Lord of all that is. He summons this particular race not because it is better or more pious or more loyal than another. On the contrary, over and over again it proves itself disobedient, hard-hearted, and inconstant. What God founded with the Hebrew people was neither a powerful theocracy nor a religion expressive of a particular racial existence. He simply entrusted the Hebrews with his word and his law, which they were to bear through history, ultimately to all the peoples of the earth. Why he selected the Hebrews for this task is the impenetrable mystery of his decree.

All this must be clear if the word covenant is to receive its full weight. Above all, it is no question of a natural give and take, no alliance between the divine essence and the tribal, no blending of divine power with earthly, no beginning of a history of God in the history of a race. Not until all these conceptions have been cleared away does the inconceivable reveal itself: in absolute freedom the Lord of the universe singles out a people, addresses it, and enables it to respond; he gives it his loyalty and demands its loyalty in return. He undertakes a divine task on earth and commands a race to render its services. If that race renounces its natural-historical existence in obedience to God's command, it will receive its fulfillment direct from divine sovereignty.

But the Hebrew people declined. They clung fast to their racial consciousness and will and hardened themselves therein. When God's Son, whose coming had been foretold throughout the centuries, comes to fulfill and end the covenant, his relation to men again assumes the form of a covenant. The people of the first covenant crowns its disobedience by turning on the Messiah and killing him; and the second covenant, which should have been sealed in faith and love, once again is sealed in sacrificial blood—now the blood of Jesus Christ. For the Messiah accepts the destiny prepared for him by the disobedient people of the first covenant and turns it into the sacrificial offering of the second, which binds the Father, Lord of the world, to his new people, now no longer a natural ethnic one, but a spiritual people, comprised by all the races of the earth and united by faith. Wherever a man opens his heart to the tidings of Christ and believes in him, he becomes a member of that "people," as St. Peter says in his first Epistle: "You, however, are a chosen race, a royal priesthood, a holy nation, a purchased people; that you may proclaim the perfections of him who has called you out of the darkness into his marvelous light" (1 Pt 2:9).

The new covenant embraces a divine people which takes nothing from any earthly people and disturbs no national history, because it exists on an entirely different plane.

It is strange how completely the idea of the covenant has vanished from the Christian consciousness. We do mention it, but it seems to have lost its meaning for us; our Christian existence is determined by concepts of the new life, the new world, God's kingdom, all of which tend to attach themselves to corresponding concepts in the natural order and to masquerade as things self-understood. But the moment of unmasking always arrives. Then the seeming naturalness of the Christian conceptions falls, and we realize with a start that Christian being is no mere continuation of natural being, that the Christian order of existence is not simply a higher step in the order of nature and man but "descends" to us from divine freedom and is meant to be caught up and held in human freedom. God summons man before him. Upon hearing the divine command and question, man is meant to liberate himself from what is purely of this earth and to prove his loyalty to God—straight *through* the ties of the world. What then takes place is based not on nature, or the processes of history, or the unfolding of the mind and spirit, but on grace, summons, freedom, decision, and all contained in the idea of the covenant. We are Christians because of a covenant. This thought must complement the other, more familiar concept of rebirth and the new creation. Covenant and rebirth: individual dignity and responsibility, and the abundance of the new life. The two great concepts belong together, for they mutually sustain one another.

Holy Mass is the commemoration of God's new covenant with men. Awareness of this gives the celebration an added significance that is most salutary. To keep this thought in mind is to remind ourselves that Christ's sacrificial death opened for us the new heaven and the new earth; that there exists between him and us a contract based not on nature or talent or religious capacity but on grace and freedom; that it is binding from person to person, loyalty to loyalty. At every Mass we should reaffirm that contract and consciously take our stand in it.

32. THE MASS AND CHRIST'S RETURN

"But I say to you, I will not drink henceforth of this fruit of the vine, until that day when I shall drink it new with you in the kingdom of my Father" (Mt 26:29). Like the concept of the covenant, which we have just discussed, this word of Christ too has been strangely neglected. Before closing these meditations let us turn our attention to it. St. Luke places the passage after the offering of the last of the Passover cups and before the words that actually institute the Eucharist. Jesus seems to be gazing through and beyond the hour of the Last Supper to the coming of the kingdom. He is referring to the future eternal fulfillment that lies somewhere behind the inevitable death toward which, in obedience to his Father's will, he now must stride. The passage tinges the whole memorial with a singular radiance which seems largely to have faded from the Christian consciousness.

It might be objected that this word was perhaps important to Jesus personally but not for his Eucharistic memorial; that before his death the Lord's vision, grave and knowing, reached across the future to the end of all things; that this thought was part of the subjective experience of the hour but has nothing to do with the sacred act which henceforth is to stand at the core of Christian life. But what St. Paul writes of the establishment of the Eucharist overturns all such theories: "For I myself have received from the Lord (what I also delivered to you), that the Lord Jesus, on the night in which he was betrayed, took bread, and giving thanks broke, and said,

'This is my body which shall be given up for you; do this in remembrance of me.' In like manner also the cup, after he had supped, saying, 'This cup is the new covenant in my blood; do this as often as you drink it, in remembrance of me.' For as often as you shall eat this bread and drink this cup, you proclaim the death of the Lord until he comes" (1 Cor 11:23–26). Can anyone still speak seriously of a mere expression of Jesus' passing mood? Specifically St. Paul connects the last things with the celebration of the Lord's memorial, and we must not forget that the Apostle's epistles are at least as early, some of them earlier, than the Gospels, and that they voice the powerful religious consciousness of the first congregations.

From all this it is apparent that when the Lord instituted the Eucharist things appeared before his inner vision more or less as follows: He knew that on the next day he would die. He knew, furthermore, that one day he would return; though "of that day and hour no one knows, not even the angels of heaven, but the Father only" (Mt 24:36). For the period between these two events he was establishing the memorial of his redemptory death. This was to be the strength and comfort of the oppressed (indeed of all who looked forward to his coming) and a constant reminder of his glorious promise. Compared to that fulfillment, passing time with all its self-importance is really only a marking time before the essential. Holy Mass is distinctly eschatological, and we should be much more concerned about our forgetfulness of the fact. But what is this "eschatological" that we meet so frequently in the newer literature? It is that which pertains to the last things, and it exists in a "natural" form in our consciousness of the fundamental uncertainty of existence. By this we do not mean any superficial uncertainty connected with our personal existence or with general existence, though this is of course part of it, but the underlying uncertainty of all existence. There are certain individuals who know nothing of this. In fact, it has been ignored by all in certain periods. For them the world is an unshakeable reality—*the* reality, essential and self-understood. Everything in it is regulated by a definite order of things, everything has its obvious causes and sure results, its clear, universally recognized value. But at certain periods all this changes. Usage seems to lose its validity. The whole structure of human society is shaken. Then accepted standards of work and propriety, the canons of taste, and the rules of behavior grow uncertain. It is no longer possible to plan the future, for everything has become fluent. A feeling of universal danger creeps into man's consciousness and establishes itself there, resulting in forms of experience peculiar to persons of a certain sensibility. What seems self-understood to those firmly implanted in action and property appears to these singularly perceptive natures as thoroughly questionable. For them the existing order of things, indeed of life itself seems but loosely, precariously balanced across the chaos of existence and its uncontrollable forces. All rules seem temporary and threaten to give way at any moment. Things themselves appear now shadowy, now ominous. Reality is by no means as substantial as it may seem, and personal existence, like all existence, is surrounded by and suspended over the powerful and perilous void from which at any instant the monstrous may rise to embrace us. To such nature's revolution, catastrophe—*Untergang*—are not distant possibilities but an integral part of existence.

It is easy to reply that such feelings are typical of the emotional crises that accompany historical turning-points and periods of personal turmoil; or that they are the reactions of an unsound, if not abnormal nature. This is possible; but it is also possible that they express something completely "normal"—the truth. The sense of the uncertainty of existence is just as well-founded as that of its opposite—that of the certainty of existence. Only the two forms of experience together contain the whole truth. These vague sensations so difficult to express and still more difficult to interpret receive their clear significance from revelation, which warns us that all is certainly not well with the world; that on the contrary, human nature is profoundly disordered; that its seeming health and stability are questionable precisely because they conceal that disorder. It revealed itself openly when the Creator and Lord of the world "came unto his own; and his own received him not" (Jn 1:11). Instead, they did everything possible to destroy him. True, his death did redeem the world; within his love a new, real protection and an eternally stable order did come into being; nevertheless, the stain of the world's turning on its God and crushing him remains. He whom the world attempted to destroy will come again, to end it and to judge it. No one knows when, but come he will. Though we cannot imagine such a thing, the world will perish, and not by its own folly or from any "natural" cause. Christ will put an end to it in the age and hour "which the Father has fixed by his own authority" (Acts 1:7). Thus Christian existence must face the constant possibility of a sudden end, irrespective of life's apparent security, order, and promise. Now we begin to see what those sensations of uncertainty really mean: threat from the periphery of time, from Christ, who will come "to judge the living and the dead," as we say in the *Credo*. The memorial of his suffering and redemption, which he placed at the heart of our present existence, is oriented toward that Coming. It reminds us how things really stand with us.

Early Christianity was acutely conscious of this situation. We see this in references to it in the Acts and feel it in the Epistles of St. Paul. Even the Apocalypse, written at the turn of the century, ends with the words of expectation: "And the Spirit and the bride say, 'Come!' And let him who hears say, 'Come!' . . . he who testifies to these things says, 'It is true, I come quickly!' 'Amen! Come, Lord Jesus!'" In other very early Christian writings as well there is a great sense of expectancy. The Lord will return and soon.

Then gradually the feeling that his coming is imminent disappears, and the faithful settle down for a longer period. However, while the persecutions lasted, in other words, well into the fourth century, existence was so precarious that the sense of the unreality of earthly things was kept very much alive. Then Christianity became the official state religion, the solid, accepted form of life, and the sense of general insecurity vanished. As we have seen, it reappears in periods of historical upset and in certain particular natures, but it no longer determines the Christian bearing as such. Thus Christian existence has lost its eschatological quality, very much to its detriment; because with that loss the sense of belonging to the world becomes more or less self-understood. Christianity's intrinsic watchfulness and readiness are gone. It forgets that the words, "watch and pray" are meant not only morally, as a vital sense of responsibility to the divine will, but also essentially, as a manner of being. The Christian is never meant to settle down in the world or become "one with nature," or with business or art. This does not mean at all negation of the world or hostility to life. The Christian is deeply conscious of earth's grandeur and beauty; he accomplishes his given tasks here as efficiently and responsibly as anyone else. What it does mean is a certain attitude toward the world. Whatever his class, the Christian is never "bourgeois," is never satiated and secure and smug. Essentially a soldier, he is always on the lookout. He has sharper ears and hears an undertone that others miss; his eyes see things in a particularly candid light, and he senses something to which others are insensible: the streaming of a vital current through all things. He is never submerged in life, but keeps his head and shoulders clear of it and his eyes free to look upward. Consequently he has a deeper sense of responsibility than others. When this awareness and watchfulness disappear, Christian life loses its edge; it becomes dull and ponderous.

Then, too, Holy Mass loses one of the marks which the Lord himself impressed upon it—a mark which the early Christians were aware of. It becomes a firmly established custom, the accepted, Christ-given form in which to praise, give thanks, seek help, practice atonement, and generally determine religious existence. Then the Mass becomes "that which is celebrated in every church every day at a certain time, above all on Sunday." This is of course correct, as far as it goes—certainly not very far. Something essential is lacking.

Perhaps it will find its way back into our lives and the Mass. The different aspects of God's Word have different seasons. At times the one will fade, retreat into the background, even vanish from the Christian consciousness.

It is still there in Scripture and continues to be read in the liturgy, but the words are no longer "heard." Then the direction of existence shifts and the same words seem to ring out, suddenly eloquent. Today history is undergoing such a change. It is breaking out of its former impregnability into a period of revolutionary destruction and reconstruction. The old sense of stability and permanence is no longer strong enough to provide the mystery of existence with "the answers." We have again become profoundly conscious of life's transitoriness and questionableness. Thus even the natural situation helps us to understand St. Paul's, "For the world as we see it is passing away" (1 Cor 7:31). Anything can happen. We begin to be aware of the magnitude of divine possibility, begin to sense the reality of Christ's coming, that pressing toward us from the edge of time, "for I say to you that I will not drink of the fruit of the vine, until the kingdom of God comes" (Lk 22:18).

Jesus' words just before the institution of the Eucharist are not there by chance. The celebration of the Lord's memorial binds the present moment not only to eternity—a thought we readily understand—but also to the future; a future, however, that lies not in time but that approaches it from beyond and that will once abolish time. Christ's promise teaches us to reevaluate the present, the better to persevere in it.

How well we understand the mood that must have prevailed in the early Christian congregations. Those people knew: everything around us is uncertain, alien, edged with danger. No one knows what tomorrow will bring. Now, however, we are here, celebrating the memorial of our Lord. He knows about us, and we know about him. He is the One who dictates the apocalyptical letters: "I know thy works . . . and thy patience . . . and thy tribulation and thy poverty . . . I know where thou dwellest." The Lord "knows everything." This knowledge is our refuge. Now, at the moment of sacred commemoration, he will come to us, will be with us, and will fortify us. Whatever tomorrow may bring, it will be of his sending.

Through this sense of momentary uncertainty presses another profounder sense: awareness of the uncertainty of all human existence. This seemingly unquestionable world of ours actually carries with it a question mark. We are beginning to notice it again and to understand the sign. At any hour the Lord may return to end the world. The celebration of the Mass should always be tinged by the feeling that the world "is passing away." A temporal thing from the start, it spins before God's eternity for as long as he permits it to do so. But its essential temporality is not all; it is seconded by an acquired temporality or mortality, the extreme disorder brought about by its disobedience and injustice. Once summoned before God's judgment, the world will be unable to "stand." When that summons is to come, we do not know, hence the admonition to watch and pray so as not to be found "sleeping." All that is certain is that it will come "soon," the word signifying no simple measure of time (tomorrow rather than a year, for instance, or thirty years rather than thousands) but an essential soon, applicable to all time, no matter how long it lasts. It is the sacred soon that comes to us from the quiet waiting of Christ, pressing terrible and blissful from the limits of time upon every hour, and belonging somehow in our own consciousness if our faith is to be complete.

All this seems strange to us. We must be honest and not pretend to feel something we do not really feel. Here is a task for our Christian self-education. We must feel our way into these thoughts and must gradually make this expectancy our own. Perhaps these meditations have at least cleared away our modern prejudices against the very terminology commonly used to express the thought. Now we must really acquire the truth of the world's "passing," must practice watching, waiting, and persevering "until the Lord comes." This implies nothing unnatural but simply truth; nothing that could make us uncertain in the world, or less efficient, but only a certain accent without which our existence is incomplete.

With it Holy Mass will receive an entirely new significance. We will realize how essential it is for us, and it will become an hour of profoundest tranquility and assurance. Throughout the noise and tension of the day, thought of the Mass will sustain us. The mind will reach out to it like a hand stretched out, each time to receive new strength.

Notes

1. Stillness

1. At this point attention must be drawn to a subject which, though only indirectly related to this chapter, is nevertheless essential to the book as a whole. We mentioned moments of stillness in the continuity of the sacred action; hence the question automatically arises: When do such moments come into being? There are many forms of the liturgy, but we are discussing this question in relation to one particular form: to the spoken (rather than the sung) Mass. But even the spoken Mass has several forms. Thus when we say that at a certain moment there is silence, this is meant as a suggestion as to how such a Mass should be celebrated, and it should be accepted as such, even though it is impossible in a limited space to present the reasons behind the suggestion, which must be left to a future opportunity.

First of all, the opening prayer at the foot of the altar should be prayed silently. In the recited Mass it is usually spoken aloud by the priest and congregation. There are certain advantages to this, but when the practice continues over a long period of time, disadvantages become apparent. Strictly speaking, the prayer at the foot of the altar does not really belong to the Mass at all; it is the priest's personal preparation and formerly was prayed in the sacristy. Its significance seems clearest when it is prayed in silence in genuine silence. A similar silence should also fill the brief interval between each *oremus* and the formal prayer which follows; there should be a real pause, in which everyone present places his intentions before God, to be gathered up by the priest in the *oratio*. The Offertory, too, should take place in the profoundest possible stillness. Essentially it is a preparation for the sacred meal and hence should keep in the background. This is mostly simply affected by allowing silence to reign from the Offertory to the Preface, also in the moments after the *Agnus Dei* and during Communion. Finally, the Last Gospel is similarly best read silently. After the *Ite, Missa est* and blessing, the sacred action is essentially over. The prologue to St. John's Gospel was added later for more or less incidental historical reasons.

This order shifts in the sung Mass; likewise in the High Mass, in which certain texts are sung by the choir. We cannot go into the question of when silence is best here; but in the sung Mass, too, periods of stillness are an absolute necessity. Lengthy, unbroken singing is objectionable, as is continuous organ music, which drives stillness from its last possible refuge. In the course of these meditations we shall see that the periods of silence are not mere interruptions of speech and song but something essential to the sacred act as a whole and almost as important as the periods of speech.

2. The importance of stillness can hardly be exaggerated. In my book, *Wille und Wahrheit* (Mainz 1938), I attempted to show its significance for our religious life and for all personal existence, as well as to suggest how it may be attained. The book also contains other passages relevant to these meditations.

4. Composure

3. See *Wille und Wahrheit.*

5. Composure and Action

4. Refer here, as well as for other parts of these meditations, to my little book, *Von heiligen Zeichen* (*Sacred Signs*, trans. by G. C. H. Pollen [London: Sheed and Ward, 1937]).

6. Composure and Participation

5. The meaning of the part of the Mass called the Offertory is easily misconstrued. It has as yet nothing to do with the real sacrifice—Christ's offering of self in his salutary death—but is merely the preparation for the sacred banquet. What sacrifice it contains is of a very simple nature: formerly the faithful brought gifts so that from them the sacred meal might be prepared and the poor fed. This sacrifice consists then in the generosity and charity which the congregation contributes to the holy service of the altar and to their neighbors.

6. How important it is that silence really reigns! Bell-ringing during Mass has become necessary—to our shame. It is to remind the faithful that some-

thing important is soon to take place; it also implies that without the totally foreign intrusion of the bells the faithful would be unaware of the fact. Something precious—stillness—is destroyed by the sound. If the faithful were really composed, the ringing would be superfluous: any persistent wool-gatherer would be called back to attention by the thundering silence of the congregation, a far better signal than the jingling of bells.

7. See my *Vorschule des Betens*.

10. Holy Day

8. The link between the seventh day of Creation and the Christian Sunday, which is the first day of the week, will be discussed in the following chapter.

18. The Congregation and the Church

9. It is interesting that all these texts have been introduced in connection with some specific (often very minor) event, and that they were not an original part of the Mass.

Sacred
Signs

Translator's Preface

That this unpretentious little book, written so long ago as the first world war, should still be thought worth retranslating and republishing is a tribute to its value as an introduction to the liturgical life. But that so elementary an introduction should be as much needed now as then, at least in America, is a tribute also to the slow advance of the liturgical movement, if that is to be the name given to the new life now quickening in the church. Never movement moved so slowly to remain a movement. Over forty years ago St. Pius X reopened the world of the liturgy, and with all his authority as Pope and man of God urged clergy and people to enter into their inheritance. The Pope has been canonized, but has he been obeyed?

In some places, magnificently. One may say that he has been obeyed wherever the liturgy was well understood. It was from the great Benedictine Monasteries, Solesmes, Beuron, Maria Laach, that the influence spread which has worked such wonders in France, Germany and Austria. We in America hardly yet know what the Pope desired. A priest, pressed by a friend, answered that it was hard enough on the people to have to worship in an unfamiliar language without forcing on them in addition an unfamiliar music. But the people, given a little encouragement, will sing the church music with all their heart. Last Easter the Baltimore Cathedral was filled with the massive voice of the congregation pouring out Creed and Gloria, and responding to the single voice of the priest; and while the mass went silently forward at the altar, the music of the seminary choir, freed from the double load of choir and congregation, reached the worshipping heart in all its intricate beauty. In this fulfilment of the Pope's so long deferred hope the joy and satisfaction (and relief) of clergy and people alike proved how right he was.

But the new life, with its source and center in the liturgy, goes out from there in every direction. It springs up in the work of an artist like Roualt, in the pastoral work of men like Parsch, and of those French priests who are carrying the word to every soul in their geographical parishes, or laboring side by side with the workers in factory and mine, in the strong impact on Protestantism of Guardini and Karl Adam, in the confident Biblical scholarship of the French Dominicans. All are parts, as a reviewer in the "Literary Supplement" of the *London Times* put it, of "a coherent system that has gone back to the fountain head." The book under review called it a Catholic Renaissance, and the reviewer added that it was a second Reformation, which may have "among its effects the healing of the breaches caused by the earlier and less radical one of four centuries ago."

If, so far as we in America have failed to catch fire, our failure is owing rather to inability than to a defect of will. Behind the liturgy is the Bible; and Catholic education here, whatever its merits, has not been such as to make the Bible a congenial book. It is a slander to say that Catholics are not allowed to read the Bible; it is no slander to say that by and large they do not read it. Our religious education addresses itself to the intellect and the will—our "spiritual faculties." It has resulted (no mean achievement) in moral firmness and mental precision. But the formulas of the Catechism do not enable us to read the two great works provided by God for our education—created nature and the Written Word. In these are addressed not only our intelligences and our wills, but the entire human creature, body and soul, with his imagination, passions, appetites, secular experiences, the whole complex in which intellect and will are inextricably mingled. Cultivated apart, and as it were out of context, our noblest faculties may grow dry and superficial. Man being of a piece, if his appetite for beauty, joy, freedom, love, is left unnourished, his so-called spiritual nature contracts and hardens.

The Bible is literature, not science, and as literature it engages man's full nature. And external nature, as the Bible presupposes it, is not a system of forces intended primarily (if at all) for man's scientific and economic mastery. The Bible takes the ancient poetic view which rests upon direct insight. Nature is a "macrocosm," and it is epitomized in man, the "microcosm." Nature is human nature written large. It is a miraculous appearance drawn from a primordial chaos back into which it would sink were it not sustained in fleeting being by the substantial hand of God. Man and nature are inseparable parts of one creation, and our being, like our justice, is God's momentary gift.

Guardini's *Sacred Signs* was designed to begin our reeducation. It assumes that correspondence between man and nature, matter and meaning, which is the basis of the Sacramental System and made possible the Incarnation. Man, body and soul together, is made in the image and likeness of God. His hand, like God's, is an instrument of power. In the Bible "hand" means power. Man's feet stand for something also he shares with God, as does his every limb, feature and organ. The writers of the Bible had an inward awareness of what the body means. As the head and the heart denote wisdom and love, so do the 'bones,' 'reins,' and 'flesh' signify some aspect of God written into our human body. The contemplation of the body of Christ should teach us what this deeper meaning is.

The next step in our reeducation after the symbolism of the body, which once pointed out we instinctively perceive, is for modern man something of a leap. He will have to abandon or leave to one side the notions instilled into him by modern science. Symbolically, if not physically, nature is composed of only four elements: earth, air, water and fire. Earth, humble, helpless earth, stands for man, and water, air, and fire for the gifts from the sky that make him live and fructify. Combined in sun, moon, and stars, they represent Christ, the Church and the Saints, though perhaps rather by allegory than symbolism. The sea signifies untamed and lawless nature, the primordial chaos; the mountains signify the faithfulness of God.

Objects, things, are not the only symbols. Their use and function, again stretching the term, is a sort of immaterial symbol. The positions and movements of human hands and feet may symbolize God's action. Direction, dimension, are also symbolic, and so are those two philosophical puzzles, time and space, which provide the conditions of human action and progress. The course of the sun is a sign to us of time; by prayer we eternalize time; and the church breaks up the sun's daily course into three or seven canonical hours of prayer. Its yearly course, which governs the seasons and their agricultural operations, signifies to us, as it has to religious man from the beginning, life, death and resurrection, and in revealed history God has accommodated the great works of our redemption to the appropriate seasons.

The last field of symbolism the sacred signs indicate to us is one that causes us no surprise. Art from the beginning has been symbolic. The Temple of Solomon like the "heathen" temples was built to symbolize the earth, and Christian Churches are (or were) built upon the model of the Temple in Jerusalem and of its exemplar the Temple in Heaven from which the earth was modeled. The axis of a Christian Church, its geometric shape and numerical proportions, the objects used in its worship, the disposition of its windows, its ornamentation to the last petal or arc, all carry our minds to the divine meaning behind the visible form.

For the modern American Catholic, as for the modern American non-Catholic, these vast symbolic regions of nature, man and art are lapsed worlds, unknown, unbelieved-in. *Sacred Signs* furnishes us with a clue. If we pick it up and follow it we shall come, as it were naturally, to reexercise over them and in them the kingship and priesthood conferred on us by God, which also, largely, has lapsed. We shall carry, as the saying is, our religion into our daily lives, and build our houses, like our churches, about a central hearth of God's charity, remember in our entrances the double nature of him who called himself the door, and in our windows who is signified by light. Every act of daily living would again take on meaning, temporal and eternal, and we should again become the doer, which man naturally is, instead of the passive receptionist he threatens to become.

Grace Branham

Introduction

This little book has been in circulation some ten years. It was written to help open up the world of the liturgy. That world will never be made accessible by accounts of how the certain rites and prayers came into existence and under what influences, or by explanations of the ideas underlying liturgical practices. Those ideas may be true and profound, but they are not apparent in the present liturgy, and can be deduced from it only by scholarly research. The liturgy is not a matter of ideas, but of actual things, and of actual things as they now are, not as they were in the past. It is a continuous movement carried on by and through us, and its forms and actions issue from our human nature. To show how it arose and developed brings us no nearer to it, and no more does this or that learned interpretation. What does help is to discern in the living liturgy what underlies the visible sign, to discover the soul from the body, the hidden and spiritual from the external and material. The liturgy has taken its outward shape from a divine and hidden series of happenings. It is sacramental in its nature.

So the procedure that avails is to study those actions that are still in present day use, those visible signs which believers have received and made their own and use to express the "invisible grace." For this it is not liturgical scholarship that is needed—though the two things are not separable—but liturgical education. We need to be shown how, or by some means incited, to see and feel and make the sacred signs ourselves.

It strikes me that the right and fruitful method is to start off in the simplest way with the elements out of which the higher liturgical forms have been constructed. Whatever in human nature responds to these elementary signs should be fanned into life. These signs are real symbols; consequently, by making them a fresh and vital experience of their own people would get at the spirit which informs them, and arrive at the genuine symbol from the conventional sign. They might even again be caught up in the Christian process that sees and fashions the things of the spirit into visible forms, and do so freshly for themselves. After all, the person who makes the signs has been baptized, both soul and body and therefore able to understand (this was the idea) the signs as sacred symbols and constituent parts of sacrament and sacramental. Then from the practice of them, which can be gained from these little sketches (which make no claim to completeness) he could move on to a deeper understanding of their meaning and justification (see my book on Liturgical Education).

It is a real question whether something written under special circumstances, and growing out of the needs of a particular group, should be republished after so long an interval of time. There are other objections to these little essays of mine of which I am quite aware. They are not sufficiently objective; they meet no classified need. They are subjective, semi-poetic, casual and impressionistic, and all this apart from their obvious literary deficiencies. Yet it remains that basically they are right, and have a claim, consequently, in spite of sound objections, to republication. For if they do not attain the end for which they were written, at least they indicate it, and no other liturgical work comes readily to mind that does even that much any better.

One person who could do what they attempt both better and more appropriately, would be a mother who had herself been trained in the liturgy. She could teach her child the right way to make the sign of the cross, make him see what it is in himself the lighted candle stands for, show him in his little human person how to stand and carry himself in his Father's house, and never at any point with the least touch of aestheticism, simply as something the child sees, something he does, and not as an idea to hang gestures on. Another competent person would be a teacher who shares the lives of his pupils. He could make them capable of experiencing and celebrating Sunday as the day it is, and feast days and the seasons of the church year. He could make them realize the meaning of doors or bells, or the interior arrangement of the church, or outdoor processions. These two, mother and teacher, could bring the sacred signs to life.

A short article by Maria Montessori, whose work in education is so significant, made me feel when I read it, that here was both the fulfillment of these ideas and their promise for the future. Her method is to teach by actual doing. In one of her schools the children take care of a vineyard and a wheatfield. They gather the grapes, sow and harvest the grain, and, as far as they can technically manage it, make, according to the rules of the church, wine and bread, and then carry them as their gifts to the altar. This kind of learning, together with the right kind of instruction, is liturgical education. For the approach to the liturgy is not by being told about it but by taking part in it.

To learn to see, to learn to do, these are the fundamental "skills" that make the groundwork for all the rest. The doing must of course be enlightened by lucid instruction and rooted in Catholic tradition, which they learn from their courses in history. And "doing" does not mean "practicing" in order to get a thing right. Doing is basic; it includes the whole human person with all his creative powers. It is the outcome in action of the child's own experience, of his own understanding, of his own ability to look and see.

When teachers such as these, out of their own experience, give instruction in the sacred signs, this little book may vanish into oblivion. Until then it has a claim, even an obligation, to say its say as well as it can.

Romano Guardini
Mooshausen in the Swabian Alligau
Spring, 1921

1. The Sign of the Cross

When we cross ourselves, let it be with a real sign of the cross. Instead of a small cramped gesture that gives no notion of its meaning, let us make a large unhurried sign, from forehead to breast, from shoulder to shoulder, consciously feeling how it includes the whole of us, our thoughts, our attitudes, our body and soul, every part of us at once. how it consecrates and sanctifies us.

It does so because it is the Sign of the universe and the sign of our redemption. On the cross Christ redeemed mankind. By the cross he sanctifies man to the last shred and fiber of his being. We make the sign of the cross before we pray to collect and compose ourselves and to fix our minds and hearts and wills upon God. We make it when we finish praying in order that we may hold fast the gift we have received from God. In temptations we sign ourselves to be strengthened; in dangers, to be protected. The cross is signed upon us in blessings in order that the fulness of God's life may flow into the soul and fructify and sanctify us wholly.

Think of these things when you make the sign of the cross. It is the holiest of all signs. Make a large cross, taking time, thinking what you do. Let it take in your whole being—body, soul, mind, will, thoughts, feelings, your doing and not-doing—and by signing it with the cross strengthen and consecrate the whole in the strength of Christ, in the name of the triune God.

2. THE HANDS

Every part of the body is an expressive instrument of the soul. The soul does not inhabit the body as a man inhabits a house. It lives and works in each member, each fiber, and reveals itself in the body's every line, contour and movement. But the soul's chief instruments and clearest mirrors are the face and hands.

Of the face this is obviously true. But if you will watch other people (or yourself), you will notice how instantly every slightest feeling,—pleasure, surprise, suspense,—shows in the hand. A quick lifting of the hand or a flicker of the fingers say far more than words. By comparison with a language so natural and expressive the spoken word is clumsy. Next to the face, the part of the body fullest of mind is the hand. It is a hard strong tool for work, a ready weapon of attack and defense—but also, with its delicate structure and network of innumerable nerves, it is adaptable, flexible, and highly sensitive. It is a skilful workmanlike contrivance for the soul to make herself known by. It is also an organ of receptivity for matter from outside ourselves. For when we clasp the extended hand of a stranger are we not receiving from a foreign source the confidence, pleasure, sympathy or sorrow that his hand conveys?

So it could not but be that in prayer, where the soul has so much to say to, so much to learn from, God, where she gives herself to him and receives him to herself, the hand should take on expressive forms.

When we enter into ourselves and the soul is alone with God, our hands closely interlock, finger clasped in finger, in a gesture of compression and control. It is as if we would prevent the inner current from escaping by conducting it from hand to hand and so back again to God who is within us, holding it there. It is as if we were collecting all our forces in order to keep guard over the hidden God, so that he who is mine and I who am his should be left alone together. Our hands take the same position when some dire need or pain weighs heavily on us and threatens to break out. Hand then locks in hand and the soul struggles with itself until it gets control and grows quiet again.

But when we stand in God's presence in heart-felt reverence and humility, the open hands are laid together palm against palm in sign of steadfast subjection and obedient homage, as if to say that the words we ourselves would speak are in good order, and that we are ready and attentive to hear the words of God. Or it may be a sign of inner surrender. These hands, our weapons of defense, are laid, as it were, tied and bound together between the hands of God.

In moments of jubilant thanksgiving when the soul is entirely open to God with every reserve done away with and every passage of its instrument unstopped, and it flows at the full outwards and upwards, then the hands are uplifted and spread apart with the palms up to let the river of the spirit stream out unhindered and to receive in turn the water for which it thirsts. So too when we long for God and cry out to him.

Finally when sacrifice is called for and we gather together all we are and all we have and offer ourselves to God with full consent, then we lay our arms over our breast and make with them the sign of the cross.

There is greatness and beauty in this language of the hands. The Church tells us that God has given us our hands in order that we may "carry our souls" in them. The Church is fully in earnest in the use she makes of the language of gesture. She speaks through it her inmost mind, and God gives ear to this mode of speaking.

Our hands may also indicate the goods we lack,—our unchecked impulses, our distractions, and other faults. Let us hold them as the Church directs and see to it that there is a real correspondence between the interior and exterior attitude.

In matters such as this we are on delicate ground. We would prefer not to talk about things of this order. Something within us objects. Let us then avoid all empty and unreal talk and concentrate the more carefully on the actual doing. That is a form of speech by which the plain realities of the body say to God what its soul means and intends.

3. Kneeling

When a man feels proud of himself, he stands erect, draws himself to his full height, throws back his head and shoulders and says with every part of his body, I am bigger and more important than you. But when he is humble he feels his littleness, and lowers his head and shrinks into himself. He abases himself. And the greater the presence in which he stands the more deeply he abases himself; the smaller he becomes in his own eyes.

But when does our littleness so come home to us as when we stand in God's presence? He is the great God, who is today and yesterday, whose years are hundreds and thousands, who fills the place where we are, the city, the wide world, the measureless space of the starry sky, in whose eyes the universe is less than a particle of dust, all-holy, all-pure, all-righteous, infinitely high. He is so great, I so small, so small that beside him I seem hardly to exist, so wanting am I in worth and substance. One has no need to be told that God's presence is not the place in which to stand on one's dignity. To appear less presumptuous, to be as little and low as we feel, we sink to our knees and thus sacrifice half our height; and to satisfy our hearts still further we bow down our heads, and our diminished stature speaks to God and says, Thou art the great God; I am nothing.

Therefore let not the bending of our knees be a hurried gesture, an empty form. Put meaning into it. To kneel, in the soul's intention, is to bow down before God in deepest reverence.

On entering a church, or in passing before the altar, kneel down all the way without haste or hurry, putting your heart into what you do, and let your whole attitude say, Thou art the great God. It is an act of humility, an act of truth, and every time you kneel it will do your soul good.

4. Standing

The respect we owe to the infinite God requires of us a bearing suited to such a presence. The sense that we have of the greatness of His being, and, in His eyes, of the slightness of our own, is shown outwardly by our kneeling down to make ourselves small. But reverence has another way of expressing itself. When you are sitting down to rest or chat, and someone to whom you owe respect comes in and turns to speak to you, at once you stand up and remain standing so long as he is speaking and you are answering him. Why do we do this?

In the first place to stand up means that we are in possession of ourselves. Instead of sitting relaxed and at ease we take hold of ourselves; we stand, as it were, at attention, geared and ready for action. A man on his feet can come or go at once. He can take an order on the instant, or carry out an assignment the moment he is shown what is wanted.

Standing is the other side of reverence toward God. Kneeling is the side of worship in rest and quietness; standing is the side of vigilance and action. It is the respect of the servant in attendance, of the soldier on duty.

When the good news of the gospel is proclaimed, we stand up. Godparents stand when in the child's place they make the solemn profession of faith; children when they renew these promises at their first communion. Bridegroom and bride stand when they bind themselves at the altar to be faithful to their marriage vow. On these and the like occasions we stand up.

Even when we are praying alone, to pray standing may more forcibly express our inward state. The early Christians stood by preference. The "Orante," in the familiar catacomb representation, stands in her long flowing robes of a woman of rank and prays with outstretched hands, in perfect freedom, perfect obedience, quietly attending to the word, and in readiness to perform it with joy.

We may feel at times a sort of constraint in kneeling. One feels freer standing up, and in that case standing is the right position. But stand up straight: not leaning, both feet on the ground, the knees firm, not slackly bent, upright, in control. Prayer made thus is both free and obedient, both reverent and serviceable.

---

5. WALKING

Walking—how many people know how to walk? It is not hurrying along at a kind of run, or shuffling along at a snail's pace, but a composed and firm forward movement. There is spring in the tread of a good walker. He lifts, not drags, his heels. He is straight, not stoop-shouldered, and his steps are sure and even.

There is something uncommonly fine in the right kind of walking. It is a combination of freedom and discipline. It is poised, as if the walker were carrying a weight, yet proceeds with unhampered energy. In a man's walk there is a suggestion of bearing arms or burdens; in a woman's an attractive grace that reflects an inner world of peace.

And when the occasion is religious, what a beautiful thing walking can be! It is a genuine act of divine worship. Merely to walk into a church in reverent awareness that we are entering the house of the Most High, and in a special manner into his presence, may be "to walk before the Lord." Walking in a religious procession ought not to be what so often it is, pushing along out of step and staring about. To escort the Blessed Sacrament through the city streets, or through the fields, "his own possession," the men marching like soldiers, the married women in the dignity of motherhood, the young girls in the innocent charm of youth, the young men in their restrained strength, all praying in their hearts, should be a sight of festive gladness.

A penitential procession should be supplication in visible form. It should embody our guilt, and our desperate need of help, but also the Christian assurance that overrules them—that as in man there is a power that is superior to all his other powers, the power of his untroubled will, so, above and beyond human guilt and distress there is the might of the living God.

Walking is the outward mark of man's essential and peculiar nobility. It is the privilege of man alone to walk erect, his movement in his own power and choice. The upright carriage denotes the human being.

But we are more than human beings. We are, as the Bible calls us, the generation of God. We have been born of God into newness of life. Profoundly, through the Sacrament of the Altar, Christ lives in us; his body has passed into the substance of our bodies; his blood flows in our veins. For "he that eats my flesh and drinks my blood abides in me and I in him." These are his words. Christ grows in us, and we grow in him, until being thoroughly formed by him, we attain to the full stature of Jesus Christ, and everything we do or are, "whether we eat or sleep, or whatsoever we do," our work, our recreation, our pleasures and our pains, are all taken up into the Christ-life.

The consciousness of this mystery should pass in all its joyous strength and beauty into our very manner of walking. The command "to walk before the Lord and be perfect" is a profound figure of speech. We ought both to fulfil the command and illustrate the figure.

But in sober reality. Beauty of this order is not the product of mere wishing.

6. STRIKING THE BREAST

When the priest begins Holy Mass, while he is standing at the foot of the altar, the faithful, or the servers in their stead, say "I confess to Almighty God . . . that I have sinned exceedingly in thought, word and deed, through my fault, through my fault, through my most grievous fault," and each time they confess their guilt they strike their breasts. What is the significance of this striking the breast?

All its meaning lies in its being rightly done. To brush one's clothes with the tips of one's fingers is not to strike the breast. We should beat upon our breasts with our closed fists. In the old picture of Saint Jerome in the desert he is kneeling on the ground and striking his breast with a stone. It is an honest blow, not an elegant gesture. To strike the breast is to beat against the gates of our inner world in order to shatter them. This is its significance.

That world, that inner world, should be full of light, strength, and active energy. Is it? We should engage most earnestly in the search to find out how it really stands with us within. What has our response been to the grave demands made on us by duty? By our neighbors, needs? By the decisions we were called on to make? Scarcely anything stirs in answer. We have loaded ourselves with innumerable offences. Do they trouble us? "In the midst of life we are in death." We hardly give it a thought. "Awake, look into yourself, bethink yourself, reflect, repent, do penance." It is the voice of God. Striking the breast is the visible sign that we hear that summons. Let the blow penetrate. Let it rouse up that sleeping inner world. Let it wake us up, and make us see, and turn to God.

And when we do reflect, what do we see? We see our lives trifled away, God's commandments transgressed, duties neglected, "through my fault, through my fault, through my most grievous fault." A world of guilt lies imprisoned within our breasts. There is but one way to get rid of it, by the whole-hearted confession that "I have sinned in thought, word and deed against God most holy, against the communion of saints." The soul moves over to the side of God and takes his part against herself. We think of ourselves as God thinks of us. We are stirred to anger against ourselves on account of our sins, and we punish ourselves with a blow.

The blow also is to wake us up. It is to shake the soul awake into the consciousness that God is calling, so that she may hear, and take his part and punish herself. She reflects, repents and is contrite. It is for this reason that priest and people strike their breasts when they confess their sins at the foot of the altar.

Before Communion also we strike our breasts when the priest holds up for us to see the Body of the Lord, and we say, "Lord, I am not worthy that thou shouldst enter under my roof," and again, in the litany when we confess our guilt and say, "We sinners beseech thee to hear us." But in these customs the force of the meaning of the rite has been weakened, as it has been also when the Host or Chalice is lifted up, or in the Angelus at the words, "The Word was made flesh and dwelt among us." The gesture in these instances has come to mean no more than reverence or humility. Its astringency should be restored. It is a summons to repentance and to the self-inflicted punishment of a contrite heart.

7. Steps

The more we think about these long-familiar things the clearer does their meaning grow. Things we have done thousands of times, if we will only look into them more deeply, will disclose to us their beauty. If we will listen, they will speak.

After their meaning has been revealed to us, the next step is to enter upon our inheritance and make what we have long possessed really our own. We must learn how to see, how to hear, how to do things the right way. Such a learning-by-looking, growing-by-learning, is what matters. Regarded any other way these things keep their secret. They remain dark and mute. Regarded thus, they yield to us their essential nature, that nature which formed them to their outward shapes. Make trial for yourself. The most commonplace everyday objects and actions hide matters of deepest import. Under the simplest exteriors lie the greatest mysteries.

Steps are an instance. Every one of the innumerable times we go upstairs a change, though too slight and subtle to be perceptible, takes place in us. There is something mysterious in the act of ascending. Our intelligence would be puzzled to explain it, but instinctively we feel that it is so. We are made that way.

When the feet mount the steps, the whole man, including his spiritual substance, goes up with them. All ascension, all going up, if we will but give it thought, is motion in the direction of that high place where everything is great, everything made perfect.

For this sense we have that heaven is "up" rather than "down" we depend on something in us deeper than our reasoning powers. How can God be up or down? The only approach to God is by becoming better morally, and what has spiritual improvement to do with a material action like going up a pair of stairs? What has pure being to do with a rise in the position of our bodies? There is no explanation. Yet the natural figure of speech for what is morally bad is baseness, and a good and noble action we call a high action. In our minds we make a connection, unintelligible but real, between rising up and the spiritual approach to God; and Him we call the All-Highest.

So the steps that lead from the street to the church remind us that in going up into the house of prayer we are coming nearer to God; the steps from the nave to the choir, that we are entering in before the All-Holy. The steps between the choir and the altar say to whoever ascends them the same words that God spoke to Moses on Mount Horeb: "Put your shoes from off your feet, for the place whereon thou standest is holy ground." The altar is the threshold of eternity.

It is a great idea that if we go up even a common stairway with our minds on what we are doing, we really do leave below the base and trivial, and are in actual fact ascending up on high. Words are not very adequate; but the Christian knows that when he ascends it is the Lord that ascends. In him the Lord repeats his own ascension. That is what steps mean.

8. Doors

Every time we enter a church, if we but notice it, a question is put to us. Why has a church doors? It seems a foolish question. Naturally, to go in by. Yes, but doors are not necessary—only a doorway. An opening with a board partition to close it off would be a cheap and practical convenience of letting people out and in. But the door serves more than a practical use; it is a reminder.

When you step through the doorway of a church you are leaving the outer-world behind and entering an inner world. The outside world is a fair place abounding in life and activity, but also a place with a mingling of the base and ugly. It is a sort of market place, crossed and recrossed by all and sundry. Perhaps "unholy" is not quite the word for it, yet there is something profane about the world. Behind the church doors is an inner place, separated from the market place, a silent, consecrated and holy spot. It is very certain that the whole world is the work of God and his gift to us, that we may meet Him anywhere, that everything we receive is from God's hand, and, when received religiously, is holy. Nevertheless men have always felt that certain precincts were in a special manner set apart and dedicated to God.

Between the outer and the inner world are the doors. They are the barriers between the market place and the sanctuary, between what belongs to the world at large and what has become consecrated to God. And the door warns the man who opens it to go inside that he must now leave behind the thoughts, wishes and cares which here are out of place, his curiosity, his vanity, his worldly interests, his secular self. "Make yourself clean. The ground you tread is holy ground."

Do not rush through the doors. Let us take time to open our hearts to their meaning and pause a moment beforehand so as to make our entering-in a fully intended and recollected act.

The doors have yet something else to say. Notice how as you cross the threshold you unconsciously lift your head and your eyes, and how as you survey the great interior space of the church there also takes place in you an inward expansion and enlargement. Its great width and height have an analogy to infinity and eternity. A church is a similitude of the heavenly dwelling place of God. Mountains indeed are higher, the wide blue sky outside stretches immeasurably further. But whereas outside space is unconfined and formless, the portion of space set aside for the church has been formed, fashioned, designed at every point with God in view. The long pillared aisles, the width and solidity of the walls, the high arched and vaulted roof, bring home to us that this is God's house and the seat of his hidden presence.

It is the doors that admit us to this mysterious place. Lay aside, they say, all that cramps and narrows, all that sinks the mind. Open your heart, lift up your eyes. Let your soul be free, for this is God's temple.

It is likewise the representation of you, yourself. For you, your soul and your body, are the living temple of God. Open up that temple, make it spacious, give it height.

> Lift up your heads,
> O ye gates, and be ye lifted up, ye everlasting doors,
> and the King of Glory shall come in.

Heed the cry of the doors. Of small use to you is a house of wood and stone unless you yourself are God's living dwelling. The high arched gates may be lifted up, and the portals parted wide, but unless the doors of your heart are open, how can the King of Glory enter in?

9. CANDLES

We stand in a double and contrary relationship to objects outside ourselves. We stand to the world and all its contents as when God brought the animals to the first man for him to name. Among them all Adam could find no companion. Between man and the rest of creation there is a barrier of difference, which neither scientific knowledge nor moral depravity can remove or efface. Man is of another make from every other earthly creature. To him they are foreign. His kinship is with God.

On the other hand he is related to everything that exists in the world. Everywhere we feel somehow at home. The shapes, attitudes, movements of objects all speak to us, all are a means of communication. It is the incessant occupation of the human soul to express through them its own interior life, and to make them serve as its signs and symbols. Every notable form we come across strikes us as expressing something in our own nature, and reminds us of ourselves.

This feeling of our connection with things is the source of metaphor and simile. We are profoundly estranged from, yet mysteriously connected with, outside objects. They are not us, and yet all that is or happens is an image to us of ourselves.

One of these image-objects strikes me, and I think most people, as having more than ordinary force and beauty. It is that of a lighted candle. There it rises, firmly fixed in the metal cup on the broad-based, long-shafted candlestick, spare and white, yet not wan, distinct against whatever background, consuming in the little flame that flickers above it the pure substance of the wax in softly-shining light. It seems a symbol of selfless generosity. It stands so unwavering in its place, so erect, so clear and disinterested, in perfect readiness to be of service. It stands, where it is well to stand, before God.

It stands in its appointed place, self-consumed in light and warmth.

Yes, of course the candle is unconscious of what it does. It has no soul. But we can give it a soul by making it an expression of our own attitude.

Stir up in yourself the same generous readiness to be used. "Lord, here am I." Let the clean, spare, serviceable candle bespeak your own attitude. Let your readiness grow into steadfast loyalty. Even as this candle, O Lord, would I stand in your presence.

Do not weaken in or try to evade your vocation. Persevere. Do not keep asking why and to what purpose. To be consumed in truth and love, in light and warmth, for God, is the profoundest purpose of human life.

10. Holy Water

Water is a mysterious thing. It is so clear and frictionless, so "modest," as St. Francis called it. It hardly pretends to any character of its own. It seems to have no other end or object than to be of service, to cleanse what is soiled and to refresh what is dry.

But at some time you must have gazed down into the still depths of a great body of water, and felt it tugging to draw you in, and have got a glimpse of the strange and secret thing water is, and of the marvels, terrors and enticements that lurk in its depths. Or, at another time when it was whipped to a boiling torrent by a storm, you have heard it rushing and roaring, rushing and roaring, and watched the sucking vortex of a whirlpool and felt a force so grim and dreary that you had to tear your thoughts away.

It is indeed a strange element. On the one hand smooth and transparent, as if it hardly existed in its own right, ready at hand to wash away dirt and satisfy thirst; and on the other a restless, foundationless, enigmatic force that entices us on to destruction. It is a proper image for the secret ground-source from which life issues and back into which death recalls it. It is an apt image for this life of ours that looks so clear and is so inexplicable.

It is plain why the church uses water as the sign and the bearer of the divine life of grace. We emerge from the waters of baptism into a new life, born again of water and the Holy Ghost. In those same waters the old man was destroyed and put to death.

With this elemental element, that yields no answer to our questioning, with this transparent, frictionless, fecund fluid, this symbol and means of the supernatural life of grace, we make on ourselves, from forehead to breast, from shoulder to shoulder, the sign of the cross.

By her consecration of it, the Church has freed water from the dark powers that sleep in it. This is not a form of language. Anyone whose perceptions have not been blunted must be aware of the powers of natural magic inherent in water. And are they only natural powers? Is there not present also a dark and preternatural power? In nature, for all her richness and beauty, there is something demonic. City life has so deadened our senses that we have lost our perception of it. But the Church knows it is there. She "exorcises" out of water those divinities that are at enmity with God. She blesses it and asks God to make of it a vehicle of his grace. Therefore the Christian when he enters church moistens forehead, breast and shoulders, all his person, with the clean and cleansing water in order to make clean his soul. It is a pleasing custom that brings grace and nature freed from sin, and man, who so longs for cleanness, into the unity of the sign of the cross.

At evening also we sign ourselves in holy water. Night, as the proverb says, is no friend to man. Our human nature is formed and fashioned for light. Just before we give ourselves over into the power of sleep and darkness, and the light of day and consciousness is extinguished, there is a satisfaction in making the sign of the cross on ourselves with holy water. Holy water is the symbol of nature set free from sin. May God protect us from every form of darkness! And at morning, when we emerge again out of sleep, darkness and unconsciousness, and life begins afresh, we do the same thing. But in the morning it is to remind ourselves of that holy water from which we have issued into the light of Christ. The soul redeemed and nature redeemed encounter one another in the sign of the cross.

11. Fire

Some cold, dull day in late autumn, when darkness is coming on, and the wide plain below as far as eye can reach is empty of life, and the mountain-path chill underfoot, and we are feeling very much alone, a strong natural desire comes over us for human contact. Then, suddenly, at a turn of the road, a light beams out. It comes like the answer to a summons, like a thing expectation called for, like a missing link in a series suddenly supplied.

Or, you are sitting at dusk in a dreary room between blank walls among uncongenial furniture. A familiar step approaches, a practiced hand sets the hearth to rights, the kindling crackles, a flame shoots up and the room glows with comfortable warmth. The change is as pleasant as when a cold inexpressive face suddenly lights up with friendliness.

Fire is closely allied to life. It is the aptest symbol we have for the soul within that makes us live. Like fire, life is warm and radiant, never still, eager for what is out of reach. When we watch the leaping tongues of flame, as they follow every current of the draught, soaring up not to be diverted, radiating waves of light and heat, we feel how exact the parallel is, how deep the kinship. This fire that forces its way through the intractable material that impedes it and reaches out to touch with light the things around and make for them a center of illumination,—what an image it is of that mysterious flame in us that has been set alight to penetrate the whole of nature and provide it with a hearth!

And if this aspiring, irresistible, life of ours were allowed to express itself outwardly, if it were given the least outlet, it also would break through and burst into flame.

And with what strength it should burn before the altar where at all times it rightfully belongs! We should stand there close to the Sacramental Presence where God addresses himself to us and we address ourselves to God, concentrating our force and our intelligence in prayer and attention. We recognize in the lamp before the altar the image and representation of what our life should be. Its flame is never allowed to go out.

As material light it has of course nothing to say to God. It is for you to make it an expression of your soul, like it burning out the force of your life in flame and light close to the Holy Presence.

We cannot learn this all at once. It must be striven for. But each moment of quiet illumination will bring you nearer to God, and will carry you back among men at peace. You leave the sanctuary lamp before the tabernacle in your stead, saying to God, "Lord, it stands for my soul, which is at all times in thy presence."

12. ASHES

On the edge of the woods grows a larkspur. Its glorious blue blossom rising on its bending stalk from among the dark green curiously-shaped leaves fills the air with color. A passerby picks the flower, loses interest in it and throws it into the fire, and in a short moment all that is left of that splendid show is a thin streak of grey ash.

What fire does in an instant, time is always doing to everything that lives. The delicate fern, the stout mullein, the rooted oak, butterflies, darting swallows, nimble squirrels, heavy oxen, all of them, equally, sooner or later, by accident, disease, hunger, cold,—all these clear-cut forms, all this flourishing life, turns to a little ash, a handful of dry dust, which every breeze scatters this way and that. All this brilliant color, all this sensitive, breathing life, falls into pale, feeble, dead earth, and less than earth, into ashes. It is the same with ourselves. We look into an opened grave and shiver: a few bones, a handful of ash-grey dust.

Remember man that dust thou art and unto dost shalt thou return.
Ashes signify man's overthrow by time. Our own swift passage, ours and not someone else's, ours, mine. When at the beginning of Lent the priest takes the burnt residue of the green branches of the last Palm Sunday and inscribes with it on my forehead the sign of the cross, it is to remind me of my death.

Memento homo quia pulvis est et in pulverem reverteris.

Everything turns to ashes, everything whatever. This house I live in, these clothes I am wearing, my household stuff, my money, my fields, meadows, woods, the dog that follows me, my horse in his stall, this hand I am writing with, these eyes that read what I write, all the rest of my body, people I have loved, people I have hated, or been afraid of, whatever was great in my eyes upon earth, whatever small and contemptible, all without exception will fall back into dust.

13. INCENSE

"A nd I saw an angel come and stand before the altar, having a golden censer; and there was given to him much incense, and the smoke of the incense of the prayers of the saints ascended up before God from the hand of the angel." So writes Saint John in the mysterious book of the Apocalypse.

The offering of an incense is a generous and beautiful rite. The bright grains of incense are laid upon the red-hot charcoal, the censer is swung, and the fragrant smoke rises in clouds. In the rhythm and the sweetness there is a musical quality; and like music also is the entire lack of practical utility: it is a prodigal waste of precious material. It is a pouring out of unwithholding love.

"When the Lord was at supper Mary brought the spikenard of great price and poured it over his feet and wiped them with her hair, and the house was filled with the odor of the ointment." Narrower spirits objected. "Whereto this waste?" But the Son of God has spoken, "Let her alone. She hath done it against my burial." Mary's anointing was a mystery of death and love and the sweet savor of sacrifice.

The offering of incense is like Mary's anointing at Bethany. It is as free and objectless as beauty. It burns and is consumed like love that lasts through death. And the arid soul still takes his stand and asks the same question: What is the good of it?

It is the offering of a sweet savor which Scripture itself tells us is the prayers of the Saints. Incense is the symbol of prayer. Like pure prayer it has in view no object of its own; it asks nothing for itself. It rises like the Gloria at the end of a psalm in adoration and thanksgiving to God for his great glory.

It is true that symbolism of this sort may lead to mere aestheticism. There are imaginations in which the fragrant clouds of incense induce a spurious religiosity; and, in such instances, when it does so, the Christian conscience does right to protest that prayer should be made in spirit and in truth. But though prayer is a plain, straight-forward business, it is not the so-much-for-so-muchness which the niggardly imagination and fleshless heart of the religious Philistine would make of it. The same spirit persists that produced the objection of Judas of Kerioth. Prayer is not to be measured by its bargaining power; it is not a matter of bourgeois common sense.

Minds of this order know nothing of that magnanimous prayer that seeks only to give. Prayer is a profound act of worship, that asks neither why nor wherefore. It rises like beauty, like sweetness, like love. The more there is in it of love, the more of sacrifice. And when the fire has wholly consumed the sacrifice, a sweet savor ascends.

14. LIGHT AND HEAT

The heart's deepest need makes us long for union with God. Two paths lead to this union, two separate paths, though they end at the same goal. The first is the path of knowledge and love. This path our own souls point out to us. The other we know only because Christ has shown it to us.

The act of knowing is an act of union. By knowledge we penetrate the nature of an object and make the object our own. We mentally absorb it, and it becomes part and parcel of ourselves. Love is also an act of union—of *union* and not merely of the desire of union. It is an actual union, for so much of a thing as we love that much belongs to us. Since there are more ways than one of loving, we call this kind "spiritual" love. But the word is not quite right, since it also applies to the other mode of union by the second path I spoke of. The difference is that while this first instinctive kind of love effects a union, it does not, as the other does, join being with being. It is union by conscious knowledge and willed intention.

Does any material form exist that provides a likeness for such a union? There does; the very wonderful one of light and heat.

Our eyes, without approaching or touching it, see and take in the candle flame. Eyes and candle remain where they were, and yet a union is effected. It is not a union of mingling and absorption, but the chaste and reverent union of the soul with God by knowledge. Since, as Scripture says, God is truth, and since whoever knows the truth, mentally possesses it, so by right knowledge of him our minds possess God. God is present in the intellect whose thoughts of him are true. This is what is meant by "knowing God," To know God is to be one with him as the eye becomes one with the candle flame by looking at it.

But the light of the candle flame cannot be separated from its heat. Though again the candle remains where it was, we feel on our cheek or the back of our hand a radiating warmth.

This union of heat is a likeness for the union between us and the Divine Flame by love. God is good. Whoever loves the good possesses it spiritually, for the good becomes ours by our loving it. Just so much of goodness as we love, just that much do we possess. "God," as Saint John tells us, "is love. And he that abideth in love abideth in God, and God in him." To know, to love God, is to be one with him; and our eternal beatitude will consist in looking upon God and loving him. Looking, loving, does not mean that we stand hungering in his presence, but that to our innermost depths we are filled and satisfied.

Flame, which is a figure for the soul, is also a figure for the living God; for "God is light and in him there is no darkness." As the flame radiates light so God radiates truth, and the soul by receiving truth is united with God, as our eyes by seeing its light are united with the flame. And, as the flame radiates heat, so does God radiate the warmth of goodness; and as the hand and the cheek by perceiving the warmth become one with the flame, so whoever loves God becomes one with him in goodness. But also, just as the candle remains free and disengaged in its place, so does God abide unmoved "dwelling in unapproachable light."

Flame, emitting light, emitting heat, is an image to us of the living God.

All this comes very much home to us on Holy Saturday when the Easter candle, which symbolizes Christ; is lighted. Three times, each time in a higher tone, the deacon sings "Lumen Christi," and then lights the Pascal candle. At once every lamp and candle in the church is lighted from it, and the whole building is alight and aglow with the radiance and warmth of God's presence.

15. Bread and Wine

But there is another path that leads to God. Had not Christ's own words made it known to us so plainly, and the liturgy repeated them with so assured a confidence, we should not be bold enough to speak of it. Seeing God, loving God, by consciously turning toward him with our minds and wills, though a real union, is yet not a union of being with being. It is not only our minds and our wills that strive to possess God. As the psalm says, "My heart and my flesh are athirst for the living God." Only then shall we be at rest when our whole being is joined to his. Not by any mingling or confusion of natures, for creature and creator are forever distinct, and to suppose otherwise would be as nonsensical as it is presumptuous. Nevertheless, besides the union of simple love and knowledge, there is another union, that of life and being.

We desire, are compelled to desire, this union, and the Scripture and the Liturgy place upon our lips words that give profound expression to our longing. As the body desires food and drink, just so closely does our individual life desire to be united with God. We hunger and thirst after God. It is not enough for us to know him and to love him. We would clasp him, draw him to ourselves, hold him fast, and, bold as it sounds, we would take him into ourselves as we do our necessary food and drink, and thereby still and satisfy our hunger to the full.

The liturgy of Corpus Christi repeats to use these words of Christ: "As the living Father hath sent me, and I live by the Father, so he that eateth me, the same shall also live by me." Those are the words. For us to prefer such a claim as a thing due to us of right would border on blasphemy. But since it is God that speaks, we inwardly assent and believe.

But let us not presume on them as if in any way they effaced the boundary between creature and Creator. In deepest reverence, and yet without fear, let us acknowledge the longing which God himself has planted in us, and rejoice in this gift of his exceeding goodness. "My flesh," Christ says to us, "is food indeed, and my blood is drink indeed . . . He that eateth my flesh and drinketh my blood abideth in me and I in him . . . As the Father hath given me to have life in myself, so he that eateth me, the same also shall live by me." To eat his flesh, to drink his blood, to eat him, to absorb into ourselves the living God—it is beyond any wish me might be capable of forming for ourselves, yet it satisfies to the full what we long for—of necessity long for—from the bottom of our souls.

Bread is food. It is wholesome, nourishing food for which we never lose our appetite. Under the form of bread God becomes for us even the food of life. "We break: a bread," writes Saint Ignatius of Antioch to the faithful at Ephesus, "we break a bread that is the food of immortality." By this food our being is so nourished with God himself that we exist in him and he in us.

Wine is drink. To be exact, it is more than drink, more than a liquid like water that merely quenches thirst. "Wine that maketh glad the heart of man" is the biblical expression. The purpose of wine is not only to quench thirst, but also to give pleasure and satisfaction and exhilaration. "My cup, how goodly it is, how plenteous!" Literally, how intoxicating, though not in the sense of drinking to excess. Wine possesses a sparkle, a perfume, a vigor, that expands and clears the imagination. Under the form of wine Christ gives us his divine blood. It is no plain and sober draught. It was bought at a great price, at a divinely excessive price. *Sanguis Christi, inebria me*, prays Saint Ignatius, that Knight of the Burning Heart. In one of the antiphons for the feast of Saint Agnes, the blood of Christ is called a mystery of ineffable beauty. "I have drawn milk and honey from his lips, and his blood hath given fair color to my cheeks."

For our sakes Christ became bread and wine, food and drink. We make bold to eat him and to drink him. This bread gives us solid and substantial strength. This wine bestows courage, joy out of all earthly measure, sweetness, beauty, limitless enlargement and perception. It brings life in intoxicating excess, both to possess and to impart.

16. Linen

The altar is covered with a linen cloth. The corporal, which, as representing the winding-sheet of Christ's body, is laid under Host and Chalice, is made of linen. The priest's alb, which is always worn during divine service, is of white linen. When the Holy Bread is being distributed a linen cloth covers the Lord's table.

Good linen, strong-fibered and close-woven, is a costly material. It has the luster of fresh snow. Once when I came upon a patch of new-fallen snow lying among dark spruce trees, I turned aside and took my heavy boots another way, out of sheer respect. It is a sign of respect that we cover holy things with linen.

When the Holy Sacrifice is offered, the uppermost covering of the altar must be of fair linen. The high altar, in the Holy of Holies, represents, we said, the altar in man's soul. But it more than represents it. The two altars are inseparable. They are really, though mysteriously, the same altar. The authentic and perfect altar in which Christ's sacrifice is offered is the union of them both.

It is for this reason that linen makes its strong appeal. We have a sense that it corresponds to something within ourselves. It seems to make some claim upon us in the nature of a wish or a reproach. Only from a clean heart comes a right sacrifice. In the same measure as the heart is pure is the sacrifice pleasing to God.

Linen has much to teach us about the nature of purity. Genuine linen is an exquisite material. Purity is not the product of rude force or found in company with harsh manners. Its strength comes of its fineness. Its orderliness is gentle. But linen is also extremely strong; it is no gossamer web to flutter in every breeze. In real purity there is nothing of that sickly quality that flies from life and wraps itself up in unreal dreams and ideals out of its reach. It has the red cheeks of the man who is glad to be alive and the firm grip of the hard fighter.

And if we look a little further, it has still one thing more to say. It was not always so clean and fine as it now is. It was to begin with, unsightly stuff. In order to attain its present fragrant freshness it had to be washed and rewashed, and then bleached. Purity is not come by at the first. It is indeed a grace, and there are people who have so carried the gift in their souls that their whole nature has the strength and freshness of unsullied purity. But they are the exception. What is commonly called purity is no more than the doubtful good of not having been shaken by the storms of life. Purity, that is really such, is attained not at the beginning but at the end of life, and achieved only by long and courageous effort.

So the linen on the altar in its fine white durableness stands to us both for exquisite cleanness of heart and for fibrous strength.

There is a place in Saint John's Apocalypse where mention is made of "a great multitude which no man could number, of all nations and tribes and peoples and tongues, standing before the throne clothed in white robes." And a voice asked, "Who are these and whence come they?" And the answer is given: "These are they who are come out of great tribulation, and have washed their robes and made them white in the blood of the Lamb. Therefore they are before the throne of God, and they serve him day and night." "Let me be clothed, O Lord, in a white garment," is the priest's prayer while he is putting on the alb for the Holy Sacrifice.

17. The Altar

Many and various are the forces that actuate a human being. Man has the power to embrace the whole world of nature, its stars, mountains, seas and great rivers, its trees and animals, and the human world in which he finds himself, and by love and appreciation to draw it all into his own inner world. He has the power of love, the power also of hate and repulsion. He can oppose and repudiate his surroundings or refashion them after his own mind. Impulses of pleasure, desire, trust, love, calmness, excitement course through his heart in multitudinous waves.

But of all his powers man possesses none nobler than his ability to recognize that there is a being higher than his own, and to bind himself to the honor of this Higher Being. Man has the power to know God, to worship him, and devote himself to him in order "that God may be glorified."

But if the majesty of God is to illuminate him wholly, if he is so to adore the Divine Majesty as to free himself from his persistent self-seeking—if he is to slip out of himself and go beyond himself and so attain to a worship of God that is for God's glory only—then he must exert a still higher power.

In the still depths of man's being there is a region of calm light, and there he exercises the soul's deepest power, and sends up sacrifice to God.

The external representation of this region of central calm and strength is the altar.

The altar occupies the holiest spot in the church. The church has itself been set apart from the world of human work, and the altar is elevated above the rest of the church in a spot as remote and separate as the sanctuary of the soul. The solid base it is set on is like the human will that knows that God has instituted man for his worship and is determined to perform that worship faithfully. The table of the altar that rests upon this base stands open and accessible for the presentation of sacrifice. It is not in a dark recess where the actions may be dimly glimpsed, but uncurtained, unscreened, a level surface in plain sight, placed, as the heart's altar should be placed, open in the sight of God without proviso or reservation.

The two altars, the one without and the one within, belong inseparably together. The visible altar at the heart of the church is but the external representation of the altar at the center of the human breast, which is God's temple, of which the church with its walls and arches is but the expression and figure.

18. The Chalice

Years ago, and only once, I came upon a chalice. The chalice. I had of course seen many chalices, but this one was not only seeing; it was a meeting, an encounter. It was at Beuron when a kindly monk in charge of the sacred vessels was showing me the treasures of the sacristy.

The broad base it stood on adhered firmly to the ground. The stem, sharp, spare and delicately thin, seemed to lift itself with compressed force and carrying power. A little more than half way up it expanded in a knob, and then at the top, first confining its strength in a narrow ring or band in orderly compression, it broke out into a wealth of foliation, finely cut but strong, in which lay the cup, the heart of the chalice.

From this chalice I caught a glimpse of the meaning of the sacrament. The sure-footed base, the long shaft molded to carry weight, the disciplined, ingathered strength blossoming out into a cup, open but enclosed, could signify but one thing: to receive and retain.

The pure and holy vessel of the mystery receives and guards in its dimly shining depths the divine drops of the gracious, fruitful blood, which is sheer fire, sheer love.

I had a further thought, an insight or rather, an intuition. The chalice represents the created universe. That universe has but one purpose and one final meaning: man, the living creature, with his soul and body and his restless heart . . . Saint Augustine has a great saying: "That which makes a man to be what he is is his capacity to receive God and hold him fast."

19. The Paten

One morning I had climbed a high hill and was turning around to go back. Below me, in the early light, ringed around with the silent hills, lay the lake, crystal clear. Great green trees bordered it with their nobly-sweeping boughs. The sky was high and spacious. The whole scene was so fresh, so clear, that a feeling of joy took possession of me. It was as if invisible noiseless fountains were shooting up into the bright, far, distance.

Then I came to understand how a man, whose heart is overflowing, may stand with uplifted face, and hands outspread like the shallow dish of the paten, and offer up to the Infinite Goodness, to the Father of lights, to God, who is love, the world around him and within him, the silent world brimming over with life and light, and how it would seem to him that that world, lifted up on the paten of his open hands, would be clean and holy.

Thus did Christ once stand on the spiritual mount and offer up to his Father the holocaust of his love and his life's breath. On a lower eminence of that same mountain, on the foothill of Mount Moriah, Abraham performed his sacrifice. And in the same spot before this the King and Priest Melchisidech had made expiation. In the self-same place, in the first age of the world, Abel's simple offering rose straight up to heaven.

That spiritual mountain still rises, and the hand of God is still stretched out above, and the gift mounts up every time a priest—not in his own person, since he is merely the instrument, of no value in itself,—stands at

212

the altar and raises in his outspread hands the paten with the white bread on it. "Receive, O Holy Father, almighty, everlasting God, this spotless victim, which I, thine unworthy servant, offer to thee, O God, living and true, for all my countless sins and negligences, and for all those here present . . . that it may avail for my and their salvation into life everlasting."

20. Blessing

He alone can bless that has the power. He alone is able to bless who is able to create. God alone can bless.

God, when he blesses his creature, looks upon him and calls him by his name and brings his all powerful love to bear upon the pith and center of his being and pours out from his hand the power of fruitfulness, the power of growth and increase, of health and goodness. "I will keep mine eye upon you and make you to increase."

Only God can bless. Blessing is the disposition to be made of what a thing is or effects. It is the word of power of the Master of Creation. It is the promise and assurance of the Lord of Providence. Blessing bestows a happy destiny. Nietzsche's remark, that instead of asking favors we should confer blessings, is the saying of a rebel. He well understood his own meaning. God only can bless since God only is the master of life. By our nature we are petitioners. The contrary of blessing is cursing. A curse is a sentence and a seal of mischief. It is, like blessing, a judgment imprinted upon the forehead and the heart. It shuts off the sources of life.

God has imparted a portion of his power to bless and to curse to those whose vocation it is to create life. Parents possess this power: "The blessing of the father establisheth the houses of the children." Priests possess it. As parents engender natural life, so the priest begets the supernatural life of grace. To give life is the nature and office of both.

And he also may attain to the power of blessing who no longer seeks himself but in perfect simplicity of heart wills to be the servant of him Who has life in himself.

But the power to bless is always and only from God. It fails wholly if we assume it of ourselves. By nature we are petitioners, blessers only by God's grace,—just as we have the virtue of authority, of effectual command, only by God's grace.

What applies to blessing applies also to cursing. "The mother's curse rooteth up the foundations of the children's houses," that is to say of their life and their well-being.

All the forms of nature are prefigurements of grace. The power of effectual blessing, the power which the blessing actually conveys, the real, the essential power, of which our natural life is but a figure, is God's own life. It is with himself that God blesses. The divine life is begotten by God's blessing. By it we are made sharers in the divine nature by a pure gift, a grace, bestowed on us by Christ. So also the sign of the cross is a blessing in which God bestows upon us himself.

This power of divine blessings is merely lent to those who stand in God's stead. Fathers and mothers have it by the sacrament of Christian marriage. The priest has it by the sacrament of ordination. By virtue of the sacrament of baptism and the sacrament of confirmation,—which makes us kings and priests to God,—there is given to those "who love God with all their heart and all their mind and all their strength and their neighbors as themselves', the power to bless with God's own life. To each of these the power of blessing is given with such difference as the nature of his apostleship determines.

The visible representation of blessing is the hand. By its position and action it indicates the purpose of the blessing. In Confirmation it is laid on the head so that the Spirit which has its source in God may flow through it. When the hand signs the cross on forehead or breast it is in order that the divine plenitude may be poured out unstintedly. The hand, as it is the instrument of making and shaping, is also the instrument of spending and giving.

Finally there is the blessing given not by the hand but by the All Holy himself with the sacramental body of Christ. Let it be bestowed in profound reverence and subjection to the mystery.

21. SPACE SANCTIFIED

Of natural space we commonly predicate three directions—up, down, and beside. They indicate that in space there is order, and that it is not a chaos. They enable us to conduct a mode of life and move about from place to place, erect buildings and live in them.

In divine and supernatural space there is also this order of direction. It is grounded in a mystery.

Churches are built along the east to west direction of the sun's course. They face the east and the rising sun. The chord of the sun's arc runs through them. They are built to receive his first and his last rays. The sun of the supernatural world is Christ. Consequently the course of the natural sun, his symbol, governs all sacred architecture and determines all its forms and arrangements. At every line and point eternal life is kept in view.

At the reading of the Gospel the missal is moved over to the left, that is, since the altar always faces east, it is moved toward the north. As a matter of history the divine message proceeded northward from the Mediterranean region, and the memory of this fact is present. But the more profound symbolism is that the south is the region of light, and signifies the divine illumination, as the north signifies darkness and cold. The Word of God, who is the Light of the World, rises out of the light and shines upon the darkness and presses hard upon it in order to make itself "comprehended."

East to west, south to north. The third direction is from above down, from below up. When he is preparing the Holy Sacrifice, the priest lifts up first the paten, then the chalice. God is above; he is the All-Highest. "Out of the depths" the suppliant lifts up hands and eyes toward the holy hills. The bishop, when he gives his blessing, lowers his hand upon the head of the person kneeling before him; the priest, when he consecrates, upon the objects to be blessed. Creation is a downward act, blessing comes down from above, from the Holy One on High. This third direction of supernatural space is proper to the soul and to God. Desire, prayer, sacrifice ascend upward from below; grace, the granting of prayer, the sacraments, descend downward from above.

In accordance with these directions the worshipper faces the rising sun, and turns his gaze upon Christ, whom it symbolizes. The divine light streams westward into the believer's heart. West to east is the soul's orientation; east to west the rise and progress of God.

From the north the darkness looks toward the light of the divine word; and from the fiery heart of the south the divine word streams out upon the darkness in light and warmth.

From beneath upward, out of the depths toward the throne of God on high, the soul sends up her yearnings, prayers and sacrifices; and God's response in grace, blessing, sacrament, comes downward from above.

22. Bells

Space enclosed within the walls of a church reminds us of God. It has been made over to him as his own possession and is filled with his presence. Walled round, vaulted over, shut off from the world, it is turned inward toward the God who hides himself in mystery.

But what of space unenclosed, that vast expanse that stretches over the level earth on all sides, boundless, high above the highest hills, filling the deepest valleys which those hills encircle? Has it no connection with things holy?

It has indeed, and the symbol of this connection is the steeple with its bells.

The steeple is an integral part of God's house, and rises out of it up into the free air, and takes possession of all wide space in God's name. And the heavy bronze bells in the belfry tower, so beautifully molded, swing about their shaft and send out peal on peal in waves of good loud sound. High and quick, or full-toned and measured, or roaring deep and slow, they pour out a flood of sound that fills the air with news of the Kingdom.

News from afar, news of the infinitely limitless God, news of mall's bottomless desire, and of its inexhaustible fulfilment.

The bells are a summons to those "men of desire" whose hearts are open to far-off things.

The sound of bells stirs in us the feeling of distance. When they clang out from a steeple rising above a wide plain and their sound is carried to every point of the compass, and on and on to the hazy blue horizon, our wishes follow them as long as they are audible, until it comes home to us that there is no satisfaction of desire in far distant hopes, or indeed in anything outside ourselves.

Or, when the pealing bells of a mountain-built church flood the valley with their clamor or send the sound straight up to the zenith, the listener, straining to follow, feels his heart expand beyond its usual narrow limits.

Or again, the bell tones in some green glimmering forest may reach us faintly, as from a great distance, too far off to tell from where, and old memories stir, and we strive to catch the sounds and to remember what it is they remind us of.

At such moments we have a perception of the meaning of space. We feel the pull of height, and stretch our wings and try to respond to infinitude.

The bells remind us of the world's immensity and man's still more immeasurable desires, and that only in the infinite God we can find our peace.

O Lord, this my soul is wider than the world, its longing from depths deeper than any valley, the pain of desire is more troubling than the faint lost bell notes. Only thyself canst fill so vast an emptiness.

23. TIME SANCTIFIED—MORNING

Though each hour of the day has its own character, three hours stand out from the rest—morning, evening, and, half way between them, noonday, and have an aspect distinctively their own. These three hours the church has consecrated.

Of them all the morning hour wears the most shining face. It possesses the energy and brightness of a beginning. Mysteriously, each morning we are born again. We emerge out of sleep refreshed, renewed, with an invigorating sense of being alive. This newly infused feeling of our existence turns to a prayer of thanksgiving for life to him who gave it. With an impulse to action born of fresh energy we think of the day ahead and of the work to be done in it, and this impulse also becomes a prayer. We begin the day in God's name and strength and ask him to make our work a work for him.

This morning hour when life reawakens and we are more keenly aware of our existence, when we begin the day with gratitude for our creation and turn to our work with fresh creative power, is a holy hour.

It is plain how much depends on this first hour. It is the day's beginning. The day may be started without a beginning. The day may be slipped into without thought or intention. But such a day, without purpose or character, hardly deserves the name. It is no more than a torn-off scrap of time. A day is a journey. One must decide which way one is going. It is also a work, and as such requires to be willed. A single day is the whole of

221

life. The whole of life is like a day. Each day should have its own distinct character.

The morning hour exercises the will, directs the intention, and sets our gaze wholly upon God.

24. Evening

Evening also has its mystery. The mystery of evening is death. The day draws to a close and we make ready to enter the silence of sleep. The vigor which came with the morning has by evening run down, and what we seek then is rest. The secret note of death is sounded; and though our imaginations may be too crowded with the day's doings or too intent on tomorrow's plans for us to hear it distinctly, some perception of it, however remote, does reach us. And there are evenings when we have very much the feeling that life is drawing on to the long night "wherein no man can work."

What matters is to have a right understanding of what death means. Dying is more than the end of life. Death is the last summons that life serves on us. Dying is the final, the all-decisive act. With individuals as with nations the events that precede extinction in themselves conclude and settle nothing. After the thing has happened, it remains to be determined, by nations as by individuals, what is to be made of it, how it is to be regarded. The past event is neither good nor evil; in itself it is nothing. It is the face we put upon it, our way of viewing it, that makes it what it is. A great calamity, let us say, has overtaken a nation. The event has happened, but it is not over with. The nation may give way to despair. It may also think the matter through again, rejudge it; and make a fresh start. Not until we have decided how to take it is the event, long past though it may be, completed. The deep significance of death is that it is the final sentence a

223

man passes on his whole life. It is the definite character he stamps upon it. When he comes to die a man must decide whether he will or will not once more take his whole life in hand, be sorry for all he has done amiss, and plunge and recast it in the burning heat of repentance, give God humble thanks for what was well done, (to him be the honor!) and cast the whole upon God in entire abandonment. Or he may give way to despondency and weakly and ignobly let life slip from him. In this case life comes to no conclusion; it merely, without shape or character, ceases to be.

The high "art of dying" is to accept the life that is leaving us, and by a single act of affirmation put it into God's hands.

Each evening we should practice this high art of giving life an effectual conclusion by reshaping the past and impressing it with a final validity and an eternal character. The evening hour is the hour of completion. We stand then before God with a premonition of the day on which we shall stand before him face to face and give in our final reckoning. We have a sense of the past being past, with its good and evil, its losses and waste. We place ourselves before God to whom all time, past or future, is the living present, before God who is able to restore to the penitent even what is lost. We think back over the day gone by. What was not well done contrition seizes upon and thinks anew. For what was well done we give God humble thanks, sincerely taking no credit to ourselves. What we are uncertain about, or failed to accomplish, the whole sorry remnant, we sink in entire abandonment into God's all powerful love.

25. Midday

In the morning we have a lively and agreeable sense that life is starting and is on the increase; then obstacles arise and we are slowed up. By noon for a short while we seem to stand quite still. A little later our sense of life declines; we grow weary, recover a little, and then subside into the quiescence of night.

Half way between the rising and the setting sun, when the day is at its height, comes a breathing space, a brief and wonderful moment. The future is not pressing and we do not look ahead; the day is not yet declining and we do not look back. It is a pause, but not of weariness; our strength and energy are still at the full.

For noonday is the pure present. It looks beyond itself, but not into space or time. It looks upon eternity.

Noon is a profound moment. In the stir and extroversion of a city it passes unperceived. But in the country, among cornfields and quiet pastures, when the horizon is glowing with heat, we perceive what a deep moment it is. We stand still and time falls away. Eternity confronts us. Every hour reminds us of eternity; but noon is its close neighbor. Time waits and holds its peace. The day is at the full and time is the pure present.

The day being at its height and eternity close by, let us attend to it and give it entrance. In the distance the Angelus, breaking the noontide silence, reminds us of our redemption. "In the beginning was the Word and the

Word was with God. . . . The angel of the Lord brought the message to Mary, and she conceived of the Holy Ghost. Behold the handmaid of the Lord, be it done unto me according to thy will . . . And the Word became flesh and dwelt among us."

At the noon hour of man's day, in the fulness of time, a member of the human race, on whom this fulness had come, stood and waited. Mary did not hurry to meet it. She looked neither before or after. The fulness of time, the simple present, the moment that gives entrance to eternity, was upon her. She waited. Eternity leaned over; the angel spoke, and the Eternal Word took flesh in her pure bosom.

Now in our day the Angelus proclaims the mystery. Each noonday, for each Christian soul, the noonday of mankind is again present. At every moment of time the fulness of time is audible. At all times our life is close neighbor to eternity. We should always hold ourselves in that quietude that attends upon and is open to eternity. But since the noise of living is so loud, let us pause at least at noon, at the hour the church has sanctified, and set aside the business we are engaged in, and stand in silence and listen to the angel of the Lord proclaiming that "while the earth lay in deepest silence the Eternal Lord leapt down from his royal throne"—then into the course of history for that once only, but since then at every moment into the human soul.

26. The Name of God

Human perception has been dulled. We have lost our awareness of some deep and subtle things. Among them the zest for words. Words have for us now only a surface existence. They have lost their power to shock and startle. They have been reduced to a fleeting image, to a thin tinkle of sound.

Actually a word is the subtle body of a spirit. Two things meet and find expression in a word: the substance of the object that makes the impact, and that portion of our spirit that responds to that particular object. At least these two ought to go to the making of words, and did when the first man made them.

In one of the early chapters of the Bible we are told that "God brought the animals to Adam to see what he would call them . . ." Man, who has an ability to see and a mind open to impressions, looked through the outward form into the inner essence and spoke the name. The name was the response made by the human soul to the soul of the creature. Something in man, that particular part of himself that corresponded to the nature of that particular creature, stirred in answer, since man is the epitome and point of union of creation. These two things, (or rather this double thing) the nature of things outside and man's interior correspondence with them, being brought into lively contact, found utterance in the name.

In a name a particle of the universe is locked with a particle of human consciousness. So when the man spoke the name, the image of the actual object appeared in his mind together with the sound he had made in response to it. The name was the secret sign which opened to him the world without and the world within himself.

Words are names. Speech is the noble art of giving things the names that fit them. The thing as it is in its nature and the soul as it is in its nature were divinely intended to sound in unison.

But this inward connection between man and the rest of creation was interrupted. Man sinned, and the bond was torn apart. Things became alien, even hostile, to him. His eyes lost the clearness of their vision. He looked at nature with greed, with the desire to master her and with the shifty glance of the guilty. Things shut their real natures from him. He asserted himself so successfully that his own nature eluded him. When he lost his child-like vision, his soul fell away from him, and with it his wisdom and his strength.

With the loss of the true name, was broken that vital union between the two parts of creation, the human and the non-human, which in God's intention were to be indissolubly joined in the bonds of peace. Only some fragmentary image, some obscure, confused echo, still reaches us; and if on occasion we do hear a word that is really a name, we stop short and try but cannot quite catch its import, and are left puzzled and troubled with the painful sensation that paradise is lost.

But in our day even the sense that paradise is lost is lost. We are too superficial to be distressed by the loss of meaning, though we are more and more glib about the surface sense. We pass words from mouth to mouth as we do money from hand to hand and with no more attention to what they were meant to convey than to the inscription on the coins. The value-mark is all we notice. They signify something, but reveal nothing. So far from promoting the intercourse between man and nature they clatter out of us like coins from a cash register and with much the same consciousness as the machine has of their value.

Once in a great while we are shocked into attention. A word, perhaps in a book, may strike us with all its original force. The black and white signs grow luminous. We hear the voice of the thing named. There is the same astonished impact, the same intellectual insight, as in the primitive encounter. We are carried out of ourselves into the far depths of time when God summoned man to his first work of word-making. But too soon we are back where we were and the cash register goes clicking on.

It may have been the name of God that we thus met face to face. Remembering how words came to be, it is plain enough to us why the faithful under the Old Law never uttered the word, and substituted for it the word Lord. What made the Jews the peculiar and elect nation is that they with more immediacy than any other people perceived the reality and nearness of God, and had a stronger sense of his greatness, his transcendence and his fecundity. His name had been revealed to them by Moses. He that is, that is my name. He that is being in itself, needing nothing, self-subsistent, the essence of being and of power.

To the Jews the name of God was the image of his being. God's nature shone in his name. They trembled before it as they had trembled before the Lord himself in Sinai. God speaks of his name as of himself. When he says of the Temple, "My name shall be there," he means by his name, himself. In the mysterious book of the Apocalypse he promises that those that come through tribulation shall be as pillars in the temple of God, and that he will write his name upon them; that is, that he will sanctify them and give them himself.

This is the sense in which we are to understand the commandment, "Thou shalt not take the Name of the Lord thy God in vain." This is how we are to understand the word in the prayer our Savior taught us, "Hallowed be thy name," and in the precept to begin whatever we undertake in God's name.

God's name is full of hidden power. It shadows forth the nature of infinitude, and nature of him who is measureless plenitude and limitless sublimity.

In that name is present also what is deepest in man. There is a correspondence between God and man's inmost being, for to God man inseparably belongs. Created by God, for God, man is restless until he is wholly one with God. Our personalities have no other meaning or purpose than union with God in mutual love. Whatever of nobility man possesses, his soul's soul, is contained in the word God. He is my God, my source, my goal, the beginning and the end of my being, him I worship, him I long for, him to whom with sorrow I confess my sins.

Strictly, all that exists is the name of God. Let us therefore beseech him not to let us take it in vain, but to hallow it. Let us ask him to make his name our light in glory. Let us not bandy it about meaninglessly. It is beyond price, thrice holy.

Let us honor God's name as we honor God himself. In reverencing God's name we reverence also the holiness of our own souls.

Romano Guardini (1885–1968) is regarded as one of the most important Catholic intellectuals of the twentieth century. He lived in Germany most of his life and was ordained a priest in Mainz in 1910. The focus of Guardini's academic work was the philosophy of religion, and he is best known for such works as *The Lord*, *The End of the Modern World*, and *The Spirit of the Liturgy*. Guardini taught at the University of Berlin until he was forced to resign for criticizing Nazi mythologizing of Jesus and for emphasizing Christ's Jewishness. After World War II, he taught at the University of Tübingen and the University of Munich. While Guardini declined Pope Paul VI's offer to make him a cardinal in 1965, his prolific status as a scholar and teacher heavily influenced the reforms of the Second Vatican Council, especially liturgical reforms. His intellectual disciples are many, including Josef Pieper and Pope Benedict XVI.

Timothy P. O'Malley is a Catholic theologian, author, and professor. He serves in the McGrath Institute for Church Life at the University of Notre Dame as the associate director for research and academic director of the Notre Dame Center for Liturgy. He regularly teaches courses on marriage and family, sacraments, and catechesis.